Ev

In brief

Seen from above, La Serenissima is shaped like a fish in whose belly several different districts are huddled together. There are six *quartieri* – or *sestieri*, as they're called in Venice. Everything has its own unique name in Venice: the city's only piazza is the magnificent square of San Marco: all the others go by the name of *campo*. Each of the streets is known as a *calle*, and every quay is a *fondamenta*. Venice's unique character has been celebrated in the work of countless writers, and many great artists too have fallen under the spell of this timeless city and its canals. Paradoxically the best way to discover Venice is to get lost in it. Get off a *vaporetto* and wander around in the network of lanes lined with the damp walls of ancient palaces, retracing your steps when you reach a dead end. Stop from time to time to investigate museums en route, and marvel at the beauty of churches that showcase the works of Venetian master-craftsmen. Half an hour's stroll is more than enough for the landscape around you to change completely, from displays of breathtaking baroque splendor and crowded art galleries to faded residential quarters with old-fashioned bistros that come to life as night begins to fall. There is the Piazza San Marco and its wonders, Dorsoduro with its fabulous museums, Santa Croce and its tucked-away restaurants, the morning bustle of San Polo when the market comes to life, Cannaregio with its ancient ghetto, and Castello, where brightly colored washing festoons the narrow lanes. Venice is for tourists, with something for everyone, but it has its secrets too. With this MapGuide, the city is at your fingertips.

Sights you should not miss

A Piazza San Marco / Castello (west)
B San Marco / Dorsoduro (east)
C Dorsoduro (west)
D San Polo / Santa Croce
E Cannaregio / Ghetto Ebraico
F Castello (east)

E
CANALE D. SACCHE
S. ALVISE
RIO
R. DI S. ALVISE
CANNAREGIO
MADONNA D. ORTO
R. DEL BATTELLO
D.
SACCA D
MISERICO
FONDAMENTA DI CANNAREGIO
CANALE DI CANNAREGIO
GHETTO EBRAICO
SENSA
FOND. D. MISERICORDIA
PONTE DELLA LIBERTÀ
R. DI S.GIOBBE
S.GIOBBE
RIO D. CREA
RIO TERRÀ S. LEONARDO
CA' VENDRAMIN CALERGI
D
S. GEREMIA
CANAL GRANDE
R. DI NOALE
C. D. RACCHE
GLI SCALZI
FERROVIA SANTA LUCIA
S. STAE
S. GIACOMO DALL' ORIO
CA' PESARO
CA' D'ORO
Ponte della Costituzione (Calatrava)
RIO MARIN
SANTA CROCE
SAN POLO
MERCAT DI RIALT
S. CHIARA
AUTORIMESSA
S. ANDREA
P.le Roma
RIO
SCUOLA GRANDE DI SAN ROCCO
Campo S. Polo
BRIDGES
S. MARIA G. D. FRARI
S. POLO
S. SILVESTRO
RIVA D. CARBO
PAL. GRIMAN
RIO TERRÀ D. PENSIERI
NUOVO
R. DI CA' FOSCARI
GRANDE
PAL. CORNER-SPINELLI
Campo S. Margherita
CA' REZZONICO
CANAL
S. STEFANO
S. FANTI
S. NICOLÒ D. MENDICOLI
RIO DI S. BARNABÀ
LA FENICE
ANGELO RAFFAELE
DORSODURO
SAN MARCO
S. SEBASTIANO
RIO OGNISSANTI
GALLERIE DELL'ACCADEMIA
COLLEZIONE PEGGY GUGGENHEIM
STAZ. MARITTIMA
FOND. ZATT. PONTE LUNGO
C
MODERN AR COLLECTION
FOND. ZATT. AI GESUATI
B
HOTEL MOLINO STUCKY
CANALE DELLA GIUDECC
S. GERARDO SAGREDO
CAN. DEI LAVRANERI
RIO DI S. BIAGIO
FOND. S. EUFEMIA
S. EUFEMIA
PALANCA
ISOLA DELLA GIUDECCA
FOND. S. GIACOMO
FO
R. PONTE LUNGO
REDENTORE

0 200 400 m
1/ 20 000 - 1 cm = 200 m

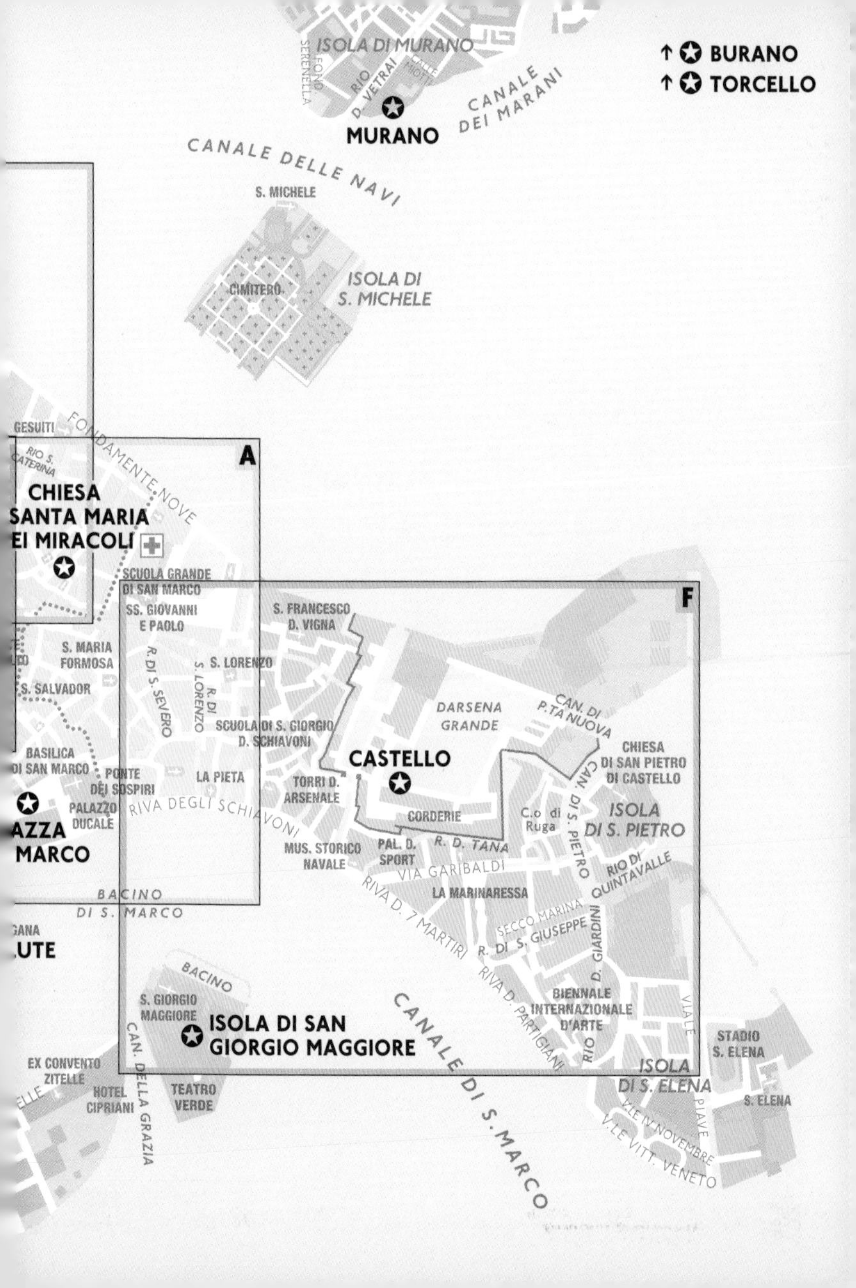

↑ BURANO
↑ TORCELLO
ISOLA DI MURANO
FOND. SERENELLA
RIO D. VETRAI
CALLE MIOTTI
MURANO
CANALE DEI MARANI
CANALE DELLE NAVI
S. MICHELE
CIMITERO
ISOLA DI S. MICHELE
GESUITI
FONDAMENTE NOVE
RIO S. CATERINA
A
CHIESA SANTA MARIA DEI MIRACOLI
SCUOLA GRANDE DI SAN MARCO
SS. GIOVANNI E PAOLO
S. MARIA FORMOSA
R. DI S. SEVERO
R. DI S. LORENZO
S. LORENZO
S. SALVADOR
SCUOLA DI S. GIORGIO D. SCHIAVONI
BASILICA DI SAN MARCO
PONTE DEI SOSPIRI
LA PIETA
PALAZZO DUCALE
AZZA MARCO
RIVA DEGLI SCHIAVONI
BACINO DI S. MARCO
UTE
F
S. FRANCESCO D. VIGNA
DARSENA GRANDE
CAN. DI P.TA NUOVA
CHIESA DI SAN PIETRO DI CASTELLO
CASTELLO
TORRI D. ARSENALE
CORDERIE
C.o di Ruga
CAN. DI S. PIETRO
ISOLA DI S. PIETRO
MUS. STORICO NAVALE
PAL. D. SPORT
R. D. TANA
VIA GARIBALDI
RIO DI QUINTAVALLE
LA MARINARESSA
RIVA D. 7 MARTIRI
SECCO MARINA
R. DI S. GIUSEPPE
D. GIARDINI
RIVA D. PARTIGIANI
BACINO
S. GIORGIO MAGGIORE
ISOLA DI SAN GIORGIO MAGGIORE
CANALE DI S. MARCO
BIENNALE INTERNAZIONALE D'ARTE
RIO
VIALE
STADIO S. ELENA
ISOLA DI S. ELENA
S. ELENA
PIAVE
V.LE IV NOVEMBRE
V.LE VITT. VENETO
EX CONVENTO ZITELLE
HOTEL CIPRIANI
CAN. DELLA GRAZIA
TEATRO VERDE

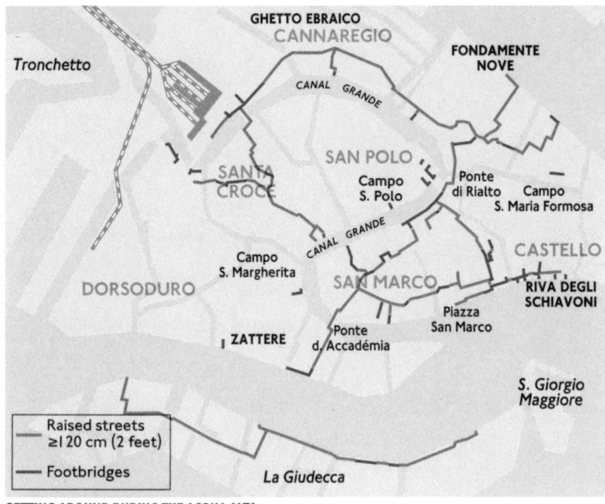

GETTING AROUND DURING THE ACQUA ALTA

→ *End Aug-beg Sep*
International film festival.
Historical boat race
→ *First Sun in Sep*
On the Grand Canal.

October-November

Garden Festival
→ *End Sep-beg Oct*
giardini-venezia.it
Discover the best of Venice's private gardens.
Venice Marathon
→ *End Oct*
Festival of the Madonna della Salute
→ *Nov 21*
Commemoration of the end of the 1630 plague.

GETTING AROUND

Venice is a cluster of narrow streets, bridges, and cul-de-sacs. Numbers do not follow each other, nor are there sides with odd or even numbers. In fact, numbers do not refer to streets but to the sections of the city. Venetians refer to the *sestiere* first (San Marco, Castello, etc.), then to the number and, finally, to the street. A church or *campo* serve as reference points.

Venetian place names

Ca' (casa): house.
Calle: street.
Chiesa: church.
Corte: courtyard.
Campo: square (except for Piazza San Marco and Piazzale Roma).
Campiello: small square.
Canale: canal.
Fondamenta: quay.
Giardino: garden.
Piscina: street or square that used to have a water tank.
Ramo: small street curved at an angle.
Rio: small canal.
Rio terrà: canal filled in and turned into a street.
Salizzada: paved street.
Scuola: former seat of a religious order.
Sottoportego: covered way.

OPENING TIMES

Beware! Most establishments close for the month of August.

Restaurants
→ *Usually daily noon–3pm, 7–10.30pm*
Banks
→ *Mon-Fri 8.30am–1.30pm, 3–5pm*
Churches
→ *Usually Mon-Sat 10am–5/6pm; Sun 1–5pm*
Churches are not open to visitors during services
Central post office (**A** A4)
→ *San Marco 5016, Calle de le Acque Mon-Fri 8.20am–7pm; Sat 8.20am–12.35pm*
Shops
→ *Mon-Sat 9am–1pm, 3–7pm*
Museums
→ *Daily 9am–6/7pm (5pm Nov-March)*
Ticket offices usually close one hour before the museums

CITY OF THE ARTS

Architecture
Different styles due to various influences and adaptations.
Venetian-Byzantine style (until end of 13th c.)
Constantinople's rival is influenced by Christian Oriental art: Basilica di San Marco (**A** B5).
Gothic (13th-15th c.)
The most typical style, with its exposed-brick façades, intertwined arches and elaborate portals: Palazzo Ducale (**A** B5), Ca' d'Oro (**E** E4).
Renaissance (15th–16th c.)
Elegance and harmony from Lombardo (Scuola Grande di San Marco, **A** C2), Sansovino (Libreria Sansoviniana, **A** B6), Palladio (Basilica di San Giorgio Maggiore, **F** A4).
Baroque (17th c.)
A profusion of theatrical ornamentation: Longhena Ca' Pesaro (**D** D1).

Painting
Giovanni Bellini (*c.* 1430–1516)
Lyrical colors and light.
Carpaccio (*c.*1460–1525)
Prodigious ability to convey a story in paint.
Lotto (1480–1556)
Delicate colorist.
Titian (*c.* 1489–1576)
From the classic esthetic ideals to tragic melancholy.
Il Tintoretto (1518–94)
Dramatic expression of light and chiaroscuro.
Veronese (1528–88)
Master of elaborate narrative cycles.
G.B. Tiepolo (1696–1770)
Greatest use of baroque style in decorative work.

WINGED LION OF VENICE

CITY PROFILE

■ Capital of Veneto ■ 342 square miles of lagoon ■ Around 24 million visitors a year ■ 58,000 inhabitants (approximately 172,000 in 1953) ■ Six districts (*sestieri*), 160 canals and 400 bridges

VIEW OF THE CITY FROM THE CAMPANILE

ACQUA ALTA

Due to the effect of the wind and the tides, Venice is submerged at high tide (*acqua alta*) between October and April. Footbridges (in red on map) enable people to walk around during flooding time, but wellington boots are necessary (newsstands sell disposable ones). As one of the lowest parts of town, St Mark's Square is routinely under water. A rarity in the 1950s, the *acqua alta* is now a regular occurrence, but the building of dams (the MOSE project) is raising hopes.

WWW.

→ *turismovenezia.it*
Website of the tourist office.
→ *comune.venezia.it*
The city's official website.
Wifi and internet cafés
Most cafés in Venice have wifi and there are a few internet cafés.
Tabaccheria 42 (**F** A1)
→ *Castello 5235, Calle Lunga Sta Maria Formosa Tel. 041 528 91 69 Mon-Sat 7am–1pm, 3.30–7.30pm*

TOURIST INFO

Tourist Office (**A** A6)
→ *San Marco, 71/F Piazza San Marco (Procuratie Nuove); Tel. 041 529 87 11 Daily 9am–7pm*
The main office; there are other branches at the San Marco vaporetto stop (**A** A6), Santa Lucia train station (**C** B1) and the airport.

TELEPHONE

Dialing codes
UK / US to Italy
→ *00 (UK) / 011 (US) + 39 (Italy) + 041 for Venice*
Italy to UK / USA
→ *00 + 44 (UK) or 1 (US) + number (minus 0 for the UK)*
Within Italy
→ *Landlines: dial the city code, including the initial 0 (i.e. 041 for Venice) + number*
→ *Cell phones: numbers begin with 333, 334, etc.*
Useful numbers
Medical emergencies
→ *Tel. 118*
Carabinieri / Police
→ *Tel. 112 or 113*
Tourist police
→ *Tel. 041 520 47 77*
Collect calls
→ *170*
American Consulate
→ *Tel. 02 290 351 (in Milan)*
British Consulate
→ *Tel. 041 522 72 07 / 74 08*
Lost and found (vaporetti)
→ *Tel. 041 272 21 79*

DIARY OF EVENTS

Public holidays
→ *Jan 1, Jan 6 (Epiphany), Easter Monday, April 25 (Liberation), May 2, June 2 (national day), Aug 15, Nov 1, Dec 8 (Immaculate Conception), Dec 25-26*
January
New Year concert
→ *Jan 1; La Fenice* (**B** E2)
Feb-March
Carnival
→ *Ten days before Lent*
Abolished at the time of the fall of the Republic (1797), the carnival was revived in 1979. It is much shorter than it used to be (ten days instead of six months), but all over the city, it more than makes up for it in intensity.
Su e Zo Per i Ponti
→ *One Sun in March*
Foot race 'up and down the bridges'.
April-May
Festival of San Marco
→ *April 25*
Gondola racing to celebrate the city's patron saint.
La Sensa
→ *Ascension Day*
City officials sail from the sea into the Lagoon to commemorate Venice's access to the sea (Sun). Fair in San Nicolo (Lido).
Vogalonga
→ *May; Sun following La Sensa*
A 20-mile regatta, from Venice to Burano and back.
June-September
Biennale
→ *June-Nov*
Fairs of architecture (even-numbered years), contemporary art (odd-numbered years), as well as dance, music and theater (every year).
Festival of the Redeemer
→ *Third weekend in July*
Fireworks over the Lagoon (Sat); religious procession and regatta (Sun).
La Mostra del Cinema

Top ten

Venice sights you should not miss

✪ Piazza San Marco (**A** A5)
Its name alone evokes all the grandeur of the ancient city. Among the marvels within are the Basilica of San Marco, the Doges' Palace and the Bridge of Sighs. For the best viewpoint try one of its two historic cafés, the Caffè Florian and the Quadri.

✪ Bridges
Venice is a maze of canals linked by more than 400 bridges. Most of them lead to private residences, such as the little Ponte Chiodo (**E** E3) or 'Devil's bridge', which has no parapet and was thought to be so dangerous that the Devil must have built it. The Grand Canal (2.4 miles) which cuts through the canal network in broad curves only has four bridges (hence the elegant *traghetti*, two-man gondolas, punting to and fro): the Accademia (**B** C3), Rialto (**D** F3), Scalzi (**E** A3) and, most recently (2006), the Ponte della Costituzione (**C** B2), designed by Santiago Calatrava. Its bold, bright outline has made it the subject of controversy ever since.

✪ Chiesa di Santa Maria dei Miracoli (**A** B2)
A Renaissance masterpiece built between two small squares at the end of the 15th c. Delicacy is the keyword here, beginning with a Virgin and Child (1408–09) by Zanino di Pietro, a statue which inspired the construction of the sanctuary.

✪ La Salute (**B** E3)
The city's most famous church was painted many times by Canaletto (1697–1768), and its imposing Palladian outline stands at the opening of the Grand Canal. Its octagonal shape resembles that of a crown and serves as a reminder that it was built in thanks for deliverance from the plague epidemic of 1630. This fact is commemorated on November 21 each year when the massive church door of St Mary of Health is opened in homage to the Virgin, in front of a long line of gondolas.

✪ Modern art collections: Collezione Peggy Guggenheim (**B** D3), **Punta della Dogana** (**B** F3)
As well as its role as cradle of the Italian baroque, Venice is famous for its Biennale and for two important museums of modern and contemporary art. Like an attraction of opposites, the city of the doges and its architecture has drawn to it important collectors of avant-garde art. Peggy Guggenheim set the scene in the 1950s with her small museum while French businessman François Pinault continued the tradition with the opening first of the Palazzo Grassi (**B** B2) and then the Punta della Dogana.

✪ Scuola Grande di San Rocco (**D** A4)
Functioning both as trade fraternities and charitable institutions, the Scuole Grandi played a key role in the social structure of the 13th c. To underline their importance, the buildings were designed by the best architects of the day and decorated by the finest painters. The Scuola Grande di San Rocco was built to help the sick, but also became an important museum of art containing, on the walls of the Sala dell'Albergo and the Sala Grande, a set of biblical canvases by Tintoretto. This immense project was executed between 1564 and 1587 by a genius at the very height of his powers.

✪ Ghetto Ebraico (**E** C2)
In 1516 the Republic banished the Jewish community to an island in Cannaregio, linked to the city by two guarded gates. Kept apart from the rest of the population for reasons of security but also to underline their inferiority to the Christian majority, the Jews were tolerated because of their great skills. As they were squeezed into an area too small to contain them properly, their dwellings were several storeys high. The origin of the word 'ghetto' comes from the Venetian *geto*, where formerly there had been foundries known as *geti*.

✪ Castello (**F**)
Each district has its own personality, and Castello appears laid back and very traditional. Outside the season of the Biennale, which is held in its public gardens, this outlying *sestiere* is a haven of peace, and authentically Venetian. Its fine traditional restaurants continue to keep the tourist shops at bay.

✪ Basilica di San Giorgio Maggiore (**F** A4)
The position of the little island (also known as the 'Isle of Cypresses') opposite San Marco gave it strategic importance from very early times, controlling access to the canals cutting through the city. On it stands a church built by Palladio in 1580, whose convent is today home to the Giorgio-Cini Foundation which has an arts center, library, open-air theater and exhibition space.

✪ Burano, Murano, Torcello
Three islands in the north of the lagoon are ideal places to spend a day. Burano, the island of lace-makers, with its colored cottages; Murano, whose glassware is world famous; and Torcello, sparsely populated and home to the Cathedral of Santa Maria Assunta, founded in 639.

Practical Venice ⤴

PONTE DI RIALTO

BURANO

GHETTO EBRAICO

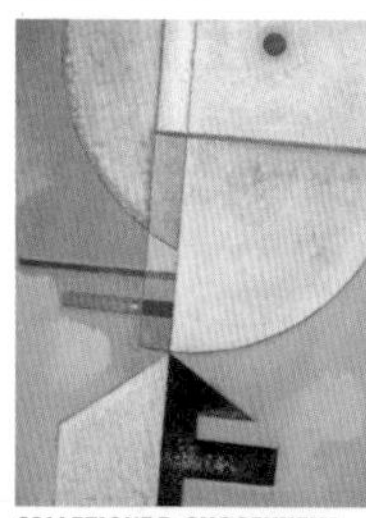

COLLEZIONE P. GUGGENHEIM

THE BRIDGE OF SIGHS

PIAZZA SAN MARCO

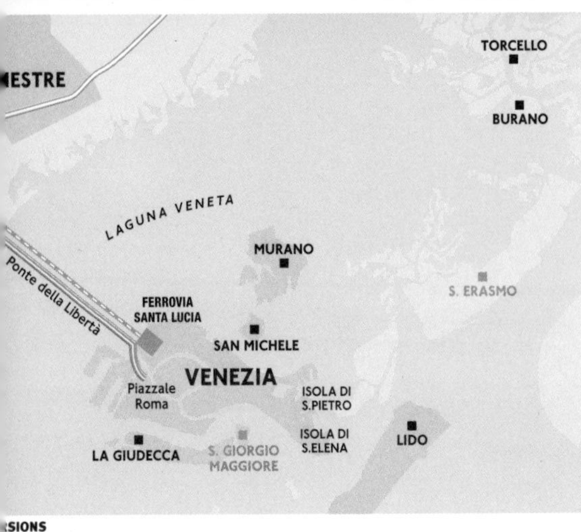

SIONS

t offices and hotels of stars; free (Ital./Eng.)
ls of music, opera heater shows, bitions, special events Italian/English).
zia News
nezianews.it
monthly magazine an/English).
rvation center
zia Unica
. 041 24 24
iaunica.it
erts, theaters
sa di Santa Maria osa dei Frari (D A4)
n Polo 3072, Campo ari; Tel. 041 272 86 11
Mecca of Venetian ed music, with jazz and then.
er for French antic Music (D B3)
lazzetto Bru Zane, San 2368; Tel. 041 521 10 05
omantic music.
sa di San Vidal (B C2)
n Marco, Campiello Vidal; Tel. 041 529 87 11
Regular concerts.
La Fenice (B E2)
→ *San Marco 1965, Campo San Fantin; Tel. 041 78 65 11 teatrolafenice.it*
The sublime opera house.
Teatro Malibran (A A3)
→ *Cannaregio 5873, Calle Corte del Milion Tel. 041 78 66 03*
One of the most famous stages in Venice.
Teatro Goldoni (D E4)
→ *San Marco 4650/B, Corte del Teatro; Tel. 041 240 20 11*
The Teatro Stabile del Veneto is based here.
Venice by night
Though dark and deserted after 10pm, Venice is safe. There are late-opening clubs and bars in Campo Santa Margherita (**C** C4), and the Rialto (**D** F3).

SHOPPING

Fashion
Designer names on Calle Vallaresso (**A** A6) and Calle Larga XXII Marzo (**B** E2).
Markets
Fish and seafood
→ *Fabbriche Nuove et Campo Beccarie (**D** E2) Tue-Sat 7am–12.30pm*
Fruit and vegetables
→ *Campo della Pescaria (**D** E2); Mon-Sat 7am–8pm*
→ *Campo Santa Margherita (**C** C4); Mon-Sat 7am–7.30pm*
→ *Rio terrà San Leonardo (**E** B3); Mon-Sat 7am–1pm*
Supermarket
Billa (E D3)
→ *Cannaregio 3660, Strada Nova; Tel. 041 523 69 70 Daily 8.30am–11.30pm*

ALTERNATIVE VENICE

Venice By Water
→ *Tel. 041 528 08 93 May-Oct: Daily 10am–6pm venicebywater.com*
For a different experience of Venice, take a kayak out along the canals or the lagoon – unaccompanied or with a guide.

EXCURSIONS

Many more treasures on the lagoon can be visited by *vaporetti*.
La Giudecca
→ *Lines 2, 4.1, 4.2*
A relaxed, working-class district opposite Zattere. At the two extremities of the island are two celebrated hotels (Cipriani and Molino Stucky) which both have nice bars.
Lido
→ *Lines 1, 2, 5.1, 5.2, 6, 10, 14, 14L, 17*
The jetset's seaside resort with luxury hotels, La Mostra palace and 8 miles of beaches.
San Michele
→ *Line 4.1 from Fondamente Nove Daily 7.30am–4.30pm (6pm in summer)*
Venice's cemetery, with its ancient pink walls. Igor Stravinsky is laid to rest there.
Murano
→ *Lines 3, 4.1, 4.2, 13*
Glassblowers' island.
Museo del Vetro
→ *Fondamenta Giustinian Tel. 041 73 95 86; Daily 10am–5pm (6pm summer)*
History of glassblowing.
Burano
→ *Burano vaporetto*
Lacemakers' island, with rainbow-colored houses.
Torcello
→ *Lines 9, 12*
Pretty, almost deserted island that was once a flourishing city.
Basilica Santa Maria Assunta
→ *Daily 10am–5pm (6pm summer)*
Splendid Venetian-Byzantine architecture (AD 639).

CAFFÈ FLORIAN

LA SALUTE

KEY DATES

697 The first Doge is elected **810** Venice becomes part of the Byzantine territory **1204** End of the Byzantine Empire, Venice becomes the hub of worldwide trade **15th c.** La Serenissima is in its heyday **Early 16th c.** New trading routes threaten Venice's hegemony **1630–31** Plague epidemic (46,000 dead) **1797** Napoleon Bonaparte abolishes the Republic of Venice **1866** Venice and the Veneto become part of the kingdom of Italy

FOOD

Avoid restaurants that display a 'tourist menu' and those where a waiter stands outside trying to tempt you in. Meals eaten at the counter are cheaper than those eaten sitting at a table.

Eating places

Bacaro: a typical bistro, where everything happens at the counter (*al banco*).
Enoteca: a wine bar that also serves snacks.
Osteria/trattoria: good, authentic, traditional food.
Ristorante: a better class of restaurant, with fancier dishes.

Glossary

Al banco: at the counter.
Cicchetto: tapas-size dish.
Crostino: toasted bread with savory garnish.
Panino: toasted sandwich.
Ombra: a glass of red or white wine at the counter.
Saor: marinated.
Spritz al bitter: the Venetian before-dinner drink (white wine or Prosecco, fizzy water and Campari or Aperol).
Tramezzino: small crustless sandwich on white bread.

Carte, menu

Traditional meals are large: following the *antipasti* (hors-d'œuvre) are two courses, the *primo piatto* (pasta, rice or soup) and the *secondo* (meat or fish) with *contorni* (vegetables), followed by *dolce* (dessert). Nowadays, it is usual to order only one main course.

Extra charges

Except when they are *tutto compreso*, prices do not include bread and cover (*pane e coperto*, around €2) or service (around 12%).
Note: *etto* means 'price for 100 grams' (an average piece of fish can weigh as much as 400 grams).

VISITS

Chorus

→ *San Polo 2986*
Tel. 041 275 04 62
chorusvenezia.org
Church visits: Mon-Sat 10am–5pm; admission €3; Chorus Pass (entry to the fifteen churches) €12
Same telephone number, opening times and entry fee for the 15 churches, this association looks after Sto Stefano, Sta Maria Formosa, Sta Maria dei Miracoli, San Polo, Sant'Alvise, San Pietro di Castello, Il Redentore, Sta Maria del Rosario (Gesuati), San Sebastiano, San Giobbe etc.

Discounts

Piazza San Marco
Admission to the Doge's Palace and the three museums on Piazza San Marco: €17.
Museum Pass
→ *visitmuve.it*
Entry to the Doge's Palace and the ten City Museums (Musei Civici): €24.
Rolling Card Venice
Concessions for 14–29 year olds: transportation, museums, restaurants etc. On sale (€4) in tourist offices and ACTV branches.
Tourist City Pass
→ *Tel. 041 24 24*
veneziaunica.it; €39.90/7-day pass (€29.90 for under 30s)
Free admission to the Doge's Palace, the ten City Museums, Fondazione Querini Stampalia, Ebraico Museum and the fifteen Chorus churches; also other reductions.

GOING OUT

Programs

Eventi e Manifestazioni
→ *Free bi-monthly (Ital./Eng.) published by the tourist office*
Listing of cultural events.
Ospite di Venezia
→ *Every two weeks, in*

CAMPANILE

MUSEO CORRER

★ **Basilica di San Marco** (**A** B5)
→ *Tel. 041 270 83 11*
Daily 9.45am (2pm Sun)–5pm
Stunning example of the Byzantine influence in Venice, the basilica with its five domes was originally built in the 11th c. to house St Mark's remains, brought from Alexandria in 828. Multiple later additions mingle effortlessly to create a magnificent architectural building. Luxurious and elaborate decor: marble tiling, 40,000 sq. ft of mosaic murals, and the Pala d'Oro (14th c.), a golden altarpiece inlaid with precious gems.

★ **Palazzo Ducale** (**A** B5)
→ *San Marco 5424, Calle Bissa; Tel. 041 271 59 11*
Daily 8.30am–7pm (5.30pm Nov-March); Book for the Secret Routes tour at muve.it or the day before in situ
The Doge's palace, a highpoint in Gothic archictecture (14–16th c.), was the ultimate symbol of the Republic, as well as a courtroom for political and legal trials. Visitors can see the courtyard and the halls displaying paintings by the Old Masters: Veronese, Palma the Younger and Tintoretto (most notably the enormous *Il Paradiso*). The guided Secret Routes tour reveals the darker side: prisons, torture chambers.

★ **Ponte dei Sospiri** (**A** B5)
Far from having a romantic origin, the 'sighs' were those of convicts crossing from the law courts to the dungeons (where Casanova is said to have escaped from in 1755), as they took their last glimpse of freedom. Visitors access the bridge when visiting the Doge's Palace, otherwise its exterior can be seen from Ponte della Paglia.

★ **Campanile** (**A** B5)
→ *Easter-June, Oct: daily 9am–9pm; Nov-Easter: daily 9.30am–3.45pm*
An exceptional view of the city and the lagoon fro the top of this bell tow (322 ft), a 16th-c. observation post that was rebuilt in 1912.

★ **Museo Correr** (**A**
→ *Piazza San Marco*
Tel. 041 240 52 11; Daily 10am–7pm (5pm Nov-M
Dedicated to the histo Venice, this museum gallery of paintings (1 16th c.) and a rich sel of neoclassical art. The same ticket allow you to visit the Museo Archeologico (featuri mainly Ancient Greec the Libreria Sansovin designed by Sansovi 1537 and boasting or

BASILICA DI SAN MARCO

PALAZZO DUCALE

A
B
1
2
3
4
RIO D. RACCHETTA
FOND. S. ANDREA
RIO DI S. ANDREA
C. ZANARDI
CALLE CORRENTE
C. DEGLI ALBANESI
POZZI
RIO DI CA' DOLCE
FOND. PRIULI
RIO PRIULI
CALLE DEL FORNO
C. DEL VERDE
C. MADONNA
CANNAREGIO
FOND. S. CATERINA
Campo dei Gesuiti
CHIESA DEI GESUITI
RIO SANTA CATERINA
RIO DEI GESUITI
CALLE
C. D. PIETA
CALLE VOLTI
CALLE VENIER
FOND. D. SARTORI
PALAZZO SERIMAN
C. D. SQUERO
C. NUOVA
C. D. VOLTO
RIO TERRÀ BARBA FRUTTARIOL
CALLE TAGLIAPIETRA
SALIZZADA D. PISTOR
C. D. FORNO
C. D. POSTA
C. D. MADONNA
C. VARISCO
C. LARGA D. PROVERBI
C. D. PRETI
CALLE MUAZZO
CALLE D. TRAGHETTO
RIO DEI SANTI APOSTOLI
C.llo Widman
PALAZZO WIDMAN
RIO TERRA
CPL. D. SALIZZADA
SANTI APOSTOLI
STRADA NOVA
Campo dei S.S. Apostoli
PALAZZO FALIER
S. CANCIANO
CALLE WIDMANN
C. D. MAGAZEN
SALIZZADA S. CANCIANO
CHIESA DI SANTA MARIA DEI MIRACOLI
CALL
C. D. POSTA
CA' DA MOSTO
PAL. BOLDU
CALLE D. MIRACOLI
Campo dei Miracoli
SQUERO
C.po S. Giov. Crisostomo
SAL. S. GIOV. CRISOSTOMO
C. CORTE DEL MILION
TEATRO MALIBRAN
RIO DI S. MARINA
PALAZZO PISANI
FONDACO DEI TEDESCHI
D. TEDESCHI
C. SCALETTA
CALLE PINDEMONTE
Campo Santa Marina
C. MALVASIA
CALLE CARMINATI
C. MARTINENGO
BORGOLOCO
C. D. DOSE
PONTE DI RIALTO
SAL. PIO X
Cpo San Bartolomeo
C. BISSA
Campo S. Lio
SAN LIO
C. D. VELE
C. DEL VOLTO
C. DEL PARADISO
F. DEI PRETI
RIO DI S. MARIA FORMOSA
RIALTO
C. D. BOMBASERI
MERCERIA 2 APRILE
C. GALEAZZA
PALAZZO GUSSONI
CALLE D. FAVA
SALIZZADA SAN LIO
C. LARGA MAZZINI
Campo Fava
RIO DELLA FAVA
C. D. MONDO NUOVO
PALAZZO DOLFIN-MANIN
Cpo San Salvador
MERCERIA SAN SALVADOR
S. MARIA DELLA FAVA
C. S. ANTONIO
CHIESA DI SAN SALVADOR
C. DE LE ACQUE
RIO S. ZULIAN
C. D. BANDE
CALLE CASSELLARIA
C. BALBI

The mythical St Mark's Square has been La Serenissima's gateway for over 1,000 years. The seat of economic, political and religious power, designed to reflect the glory of the empire, it hosts Venice's most prestigious buildings: the Doges' Palace and the Basilica di San Marco. Climb the campanile for an unparalleled view of the entire city and lagoon. Down below is the legendary Bridge of Sighs. From here, twisting alleyways lead to Campo Santa Maria Formosa, lined with ornate palaces. Further north lies Campo Santi Giovanni e Paolo and its wonderful eponymous basilica and the Scuola Grande di San Marco.

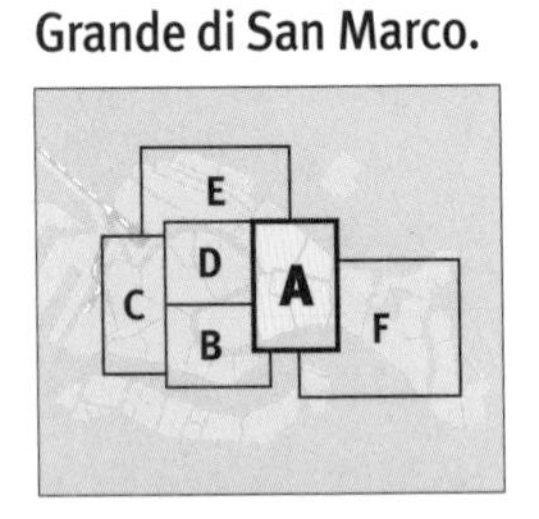

ROSTICCERIA SAN BARTOLOMEO GRAND CANAL

RESTAURANTS

Rosticceria San Bartolomeo (**A** A3)
→ *San Marco 5424, Calle Bissa; Tel. 041 522 35 69 Daily 9am–9.30pm*
Venetians have been flocking to this informal restaurant for 80 years to enjoy its generous portions of local specialties. Eat at the bar or at a table, or take away a snack: the breaded mozzarella is particularly delicious. Entrées €9–22.

Giardinetto da Severino (**A** C4)
→ *Castello 4928, Salizzada Zorzi ; Tel. 041 528 53 32 Fri-Wed noon–3pm, 7–10pm*
All the wonders of Venetian cooking in a 15th-c. palace or on the patio shaded by climbing plants: *bigoli in salsa* (pasta with sardines and anchovies), *castradina* (dried and smoked lamb). Entrées €10–19.

Da Carla (**A** A5)
→ *San Marco 1535/A, Corte Contarina Tel. 041 523 78 55 Mon-Sat 8.30am–10.30pm*
An osteria in a quiet back street, very close to St Mark's Square. The house specialties include cuttlefish, polenta and fried fish. Also, a wide range of *cicchetti*, fresh pasta and salads. Terrace. Entrées €10–25.

Da Alvise (**A** C1)
→ *Cannaregio 5045/A Fondamente Nove Tel. 041 520 15 15 Daily noon–3pm, 7–10.30pm (closed Mon in winter)*
The thin, crusty pizzas produced by this quintessentially Venetian trattoria are served on the edge of the lagoon, overlooking San Michele Island. Entrées €13–15.

Fiaschetteria Toscana (**A** A3)
→ *Cannaregio 5719, Campo San Giovanni Crisostomo Tel. 041 528 52 81; Wed 7.30–10.30pm; Thu-Mon 12.30–2.30pm, 7.30–10.30pm*
Only Tuscan by name, this family-owned restaurant owes its fame to its delicious Venetian dishes: fish from the Laguna and delicious desserts like the *rovesciat di mele al caramello* (a typ of *tarte tatin*). Superb wine list. Entrées €15–35.

Grand Canal (**A** A6)
→ *Monaco Hotel, San Marc 1325, Calle Vallaresso; Tel. 041 520 02 11; Daily 12.30–2.30pm, 7.30–10.15pm*
One of Venice's finest terraces, opening onto the Grand Canal and the church of La Salute.

/ICH

HARRY'S BAR

GIACOMO RIZZO

The food is just as fancy: swordfish tartare, pasta with langoustines. Entrées €18–36.

ICE-CREAM PARLOR PATISSERIES, CAFÉ

La Boutique del Gelato (**A** B3)
→ *Castello 5727, Salizzada San Lio; Tel. 041 522 32 83 Daily 10.30am–8pm (10.30pm June-Sep)*
One of the Venetians' favorite ice-cream parlors. *Fior di latte, tiramisù, nocciola, gianduia, stracciatella*: the flavors are as divine as their names.

Didovich (**A** B3)
→ *Castello 5908, Campo S. Marina; Tel. 041 523 00 17 Mon-Sat 7am–8pm*
The mouthwatering window display of cakes and tarts is fully realised in the delights served at the bar or in the tea room with a terrace. Savory snacks at lunchtime: small pizzas and pies.

Rosa Salva (**A** C3)
→ *Castello 6779, Campo di Santi Giovanni e Paolo Tel 041 522 79 49; Daily 7.30am (8.30am Sun)–8pm*
Typical Venetian pastries (*baicoli, bussolai* – dried aniseed biscuits) and homemade ice cream. Terrace on the *campo*.

Caffè Florian (**A** A5)
→ *Piazza San Marco 56-59, Procuratie Nuove; Tel. 041 520 56 41; Summer: daily 9am–midnight; Winter: Mon-Thu 10am–9pm; Fri-Sun 9am–11pm (9pm Sun)*
A historic café (1720) tucked away under the arcades of St Mark's Square. Sumptuous and expensive but not to be missed, if only for the coffee served on a silver tray. In summer, classical concerts on the terrace.

BARS

Zanzibar (**A** B3)
→ *Castello 5840, Campo Santa Maria Formosa Tel. 348 045 54 34; Daily 8am–2am (Mon-Sat 8am–9pm in winter)*
A tiny bar with a large sunny terrace giving onto the Campo Santa Maria Formosa.

Harry's Bar (**A** A6)
→ *San Marco 1323, Calle Vallaresso; Tel. 041 528 57 77 Daily 10.30am–11pm*
An institution, still popular with tourists and celebrities alike, more than 50 years after Hemingway created the explosive Montgomery cocktail here: 15 parts gin to 1 part Martini!

Devil's Forest Pub (**A** A3)
→ *San Marco 5185, Campo San Bartolomeo Tel. 041 520 06 23 Daily 11am–midnight*
A small corner of Ireland in a quiet Venetian back street. This pub is popular with students, attracted by its screenings of live soccer matches.

SHOPPING

Venini (**A** B5)
→ *San Marco 314, Piazzetta dei Leoncini Tel. 041 522 40 45 Mon-Sat 10am–7pm*
Stunning creations in Murano blown glass. Lamps, chandeliers and vases in bright colors and avant-garde designs.

I Love Tourism Shop (**A** A5)
→ *San Marco 71/c, Piazza San Marco, Fondazione Bevilacqua La Masa Mon-Sat 10.30am–5.30pm*
Both functional and decorative objects created by young Italian designers.

Gianni Basso (**A** B1)
→ *Cannaregio 5306, Calle del Fumo Tel. 041 523 46 81 Mon-Fri 9am–1pm, 2–6pm; Sat 9am–noon*
According to Gianni Basso, his printing shop is a living museum. Indeed, he has been making and selling prints, business cards, ex-libris and headed paper for more than 30 years on machinery dating back to Gutenberg.

Bottiglieria Colonna (**A** A3)
→ *Castello 5595, Calle della Fava; Tel. 041 528 51 37 Mon-Sat 9am–1pm, 4–8pm*
Italian wines for all budgets and occasions, as well as balsamic vinegars, liquors and *grappe* (grape brandies). Mauro, the owner, provides expert guidance.

I Tre Mercanti (**A** B4)
→ *Castello 5364, Campo della Guerra; Tel. 041 522 29 01; Daily 11am–7.30pm*
A deli selling gourmet food from all over Italy and Venetia: *grappa*, Prosecco, wine, etc.

Giacomo Rizzo (**A** A3)
→ *Cannaregio 5778, Salizzada San G. Crisostomo Tel. 041 522 28 24; Mon-Sat 8.30am–1pm, 3.30–7.30pm*
An exuberant array of homemade pasta in every conceivable color and flavor: artichoke, curry, chilli, smoked salmon, bitter cocoa, blueberry. A Venetian institution for four generations.

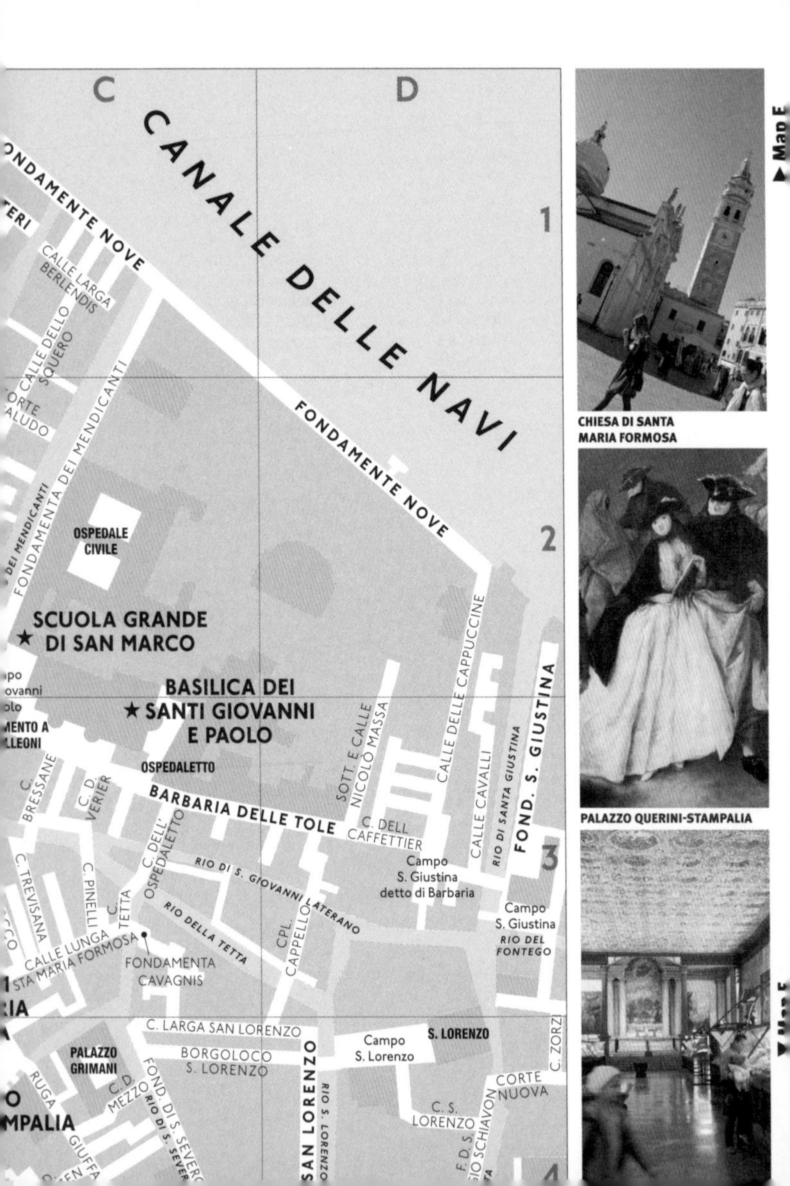

CHIESA DI SANTA MARIA FORMOSA

PALAZZO QUERINI-STAMPALIA

▶ Map E

▼ Map F

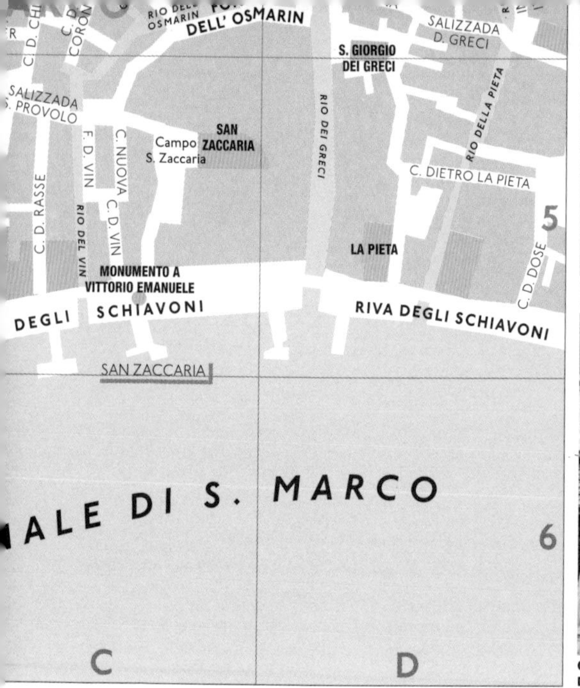

BASILICA DEI SANTI GIOVANNI E PAOLO

CHIESA DI SANTA MARIA DEI MIRACOLI

…gs painted by Titian, …ese and Tintoretto.

…esa di Santa … Formosa (A C4)
…tello 5263, Campo …Maria Formosa …at 10am–5pm
…Venice's oldest …aries. Mauro Codussi …is three-nave church …. The polyptych …by Palma the Elder …cated to St Barbara, …s the features of the …voman' of Venetian …entury painting.

…zzo Querini-…alia (A C4)
…ello 5252, Campo …laria Formosa … 271 14 11; Tue-Sun 10am–6pm (7pm Sun)
The art gallery in this Renaissance palace immerses visitors in the atmosphere of the 18th c., with a whole room devoted to Pietro Longhi (1702–85). The contemporary garden was immaculately restored by Carlo Scarpa in 1960.

★ Scuola Grande di San Marco (A C2)
→ Castello 6768, Campo Santi Giovanni e Paolo; Tue-Sat 9.30am–1pm, 2–5pm
The asymmetric, marble-inlaid façade with its broad, projecting portal and trompe-l'oeil effects make this one of the most prestigious buildings on the campo that used to be called *delle Maravege* ('of the wonders'). Founded in 1260 as a charitable and religious institution, the *scuola* is now a hospital and a museum of medicine.

★ Basilica dei Santi Giovanni e Paolo (A C3)
→ Castello 6363, Campo Santi Giovanni e Paolo Tel. 041 523 59 13; Daily 9am (noon Sun)–6pm
A subtle blend of red brick and white stone, this huge building is one of Venice's grandest examples of religious Gothic architecture (along with the Frari). Built in the 13th c. by Dominicans, it became the city's pantheon in the 1400s: there are monuments to 25 doges, sculpted by some of Italy's greatest masters, and famous paintings by Bellini, Lotto and Veronese.

★ Chiesa di Santa Maria dei Miracoli (A B2)
→ Cannaregio, Campo dei Miracoli; Mon-Sat 10am–5pm (see Chorus in Practical Venice)
A Renaissance gem (1481–89) by Pietro Lombardo. Its façade, graced by beautiful masterpieces of inlaid woodwork, is encrusted with medallions of multicolored marble. In the unique nave are fine reliefs, bas-reliefs and painted coffered vaulting.

GALLERIE DELL'ACCADEMIA

I GESUATI

COLLEZIONE PEGGY GUGGENHEIM

★ **Palazzo Contarini del Bovolo** (**B** E1)
→ *San Marco 4299, Corte del Bovolo; Tel. 041 271 90 12*
Closed for renovation works
Known for the amazing spiral staircase (1499) linking the loggias to the palace itself, this splendid building marks the transition between Gothic and Renaissance styles, and is a feat of architectural brilliance and creativity by Venetian builders. Great views of the roofs of San Marco from the fourth floor.

★ **La Fenice** (**B** E2)
→ *San Marco 1965, Campo San Fantin; Tel. 041 24 24*
Visits daily 9.30am–6pm (1pm if there is a performance)
A remarkable neoclassical theater and world-famous opera stage, built in 1792. The *fenice* or 'phoenix', destroyed by fire in 1836 and again in 1996, has risen from the ashes twice. The red and gold room is a replica of the one that first witnessed Verdi's operas.

★ **Chiesa di Santo Stefano** (**B** D2)
→ *San Marco 3825, Campo Santo Stefano; Mon-Sat 10am–5pm (see Chorus in Practical Venice)*
This church has delicate flamboyant Gothic motifs (15th c.) on its otherwise austere façade and, inside, a stunning ceiling in the shape of a ship's keel, supported by white and red marble columns. Don't miss the three paintings (1579–80) by Tintoretto in the sacristy.

★ **Palazzo Pisani** (**B** C2)
→ *San Marco 2810, Campiello Pisani*
Tel 041 522 56 04
Book at conseve.net
This colossal palace, made of Istrian stone and restored in the 18th century, hides two towers surrounded by loggias. Today it houses the music conservatory. Open-air operas and ballets are staged here in summer.

★ **Palazzo Grassi** (**B**
→ *San Marco 3231, Car San Samuele; Tel. 199 1*
Wed-Mon 10am–7pm
This palace (1748–72 of the last to be built La Serenissima, was renovated in 2006 by Ando to house temp exhibitions, most of showing works from contemporary art col of French businessm François Pinault.

★ **Ca' Rezzonico** (**B**
→ *Dorsoduro 3136, Fondamenta Rezzonico 041 241 01 00; Wed-*
10am–6pm (5pm Nov-
This monumental pa exudes all the atmos

PALAZZO CONTARINI DEL BOVOLO

LA FENICE

CHIESA DI SANTO STEFAN

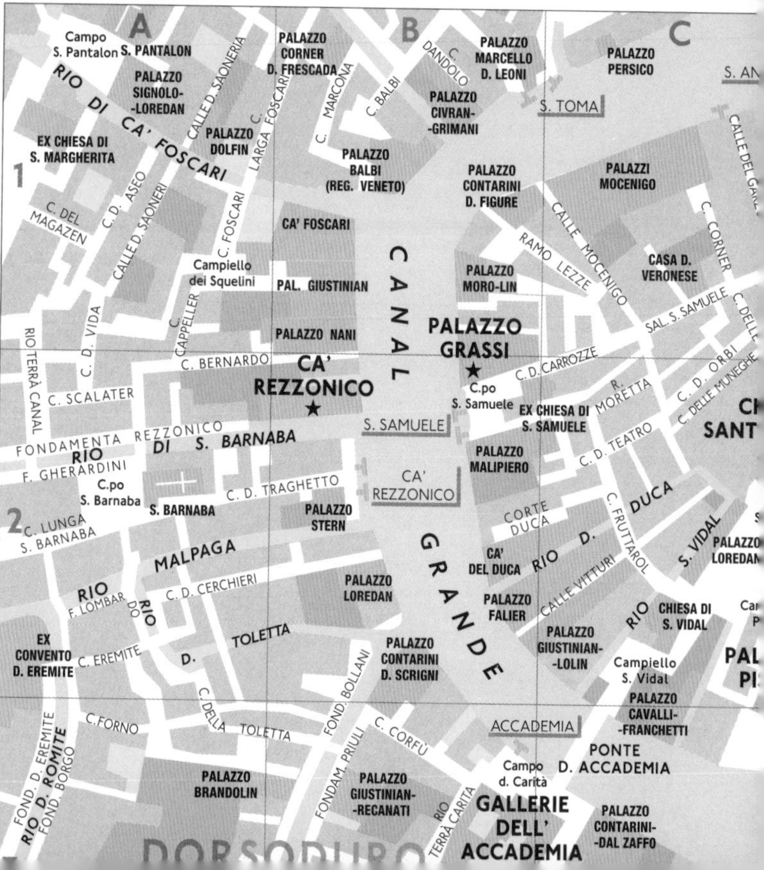

A
B
C
1
2

Campo S. Pantalon
S. PANTALON
RIO DI CA' FOSCARI
PALAZZO SIGNOLO-LOREDAN
CALLE D. SAONERIA
PALAZZO CORNER D. FRESCADA
C. MARCONA
C. BALBI
C. DANDOLO
PALAZZO MARCELLO D. LEONI
PALAZZO PERSICO
S. AN
S. TOMA
PALAZZO CIVRAN-GRIMANI
EX CHIESA DI S. MARGHERITA
PALAZZO DOLFIN
C. LARGA FOSCARI
PALAZZO BALBI (REG. VENETO)
PALAZZO CONTARINI D. FIGURE
PALAZZI MOCENIGO
CALLE DEL GARZ
C. DEL MAGAZEN
C. D. ASEO
CALLE D. SAONERI
C. FOSCARI
CA' FOSCARI
CALLE MOCENIGO
RAMO LEZZE
C. CORNER
CASA D. VERONESE
Campiello dei Squelini
PAL. GIUSTINIAN
CANAL
PALAZZO MORO-LIN
C. CAPPELLER
C. D. VIDA
PALAZZO NANI
PALAZZO GRASSI
SAL. S. SAMUELE
C. DELLE
RIO TERRÀ CANAL
C. BERNARDO
CA' REZZONICO
C. D. CARROZZE
C.po S. Samuele
C. D. ORBI
C. DELLE MUNEGHE
C. SCALATER
R. MORETTA
EX CHIESA DI S. SAMUELE
CH SANT
FONDAMENTA REZZONICO
RIO DI S. BARNABA
S. SAMUELE
C. D. TEATRO
F. GHERARDINI
PALAZZO MALIPIERO
C.po S. Barnaba
C. D. TRAGHETTO
CA' REZZONICO
S. BARNABA
PALAZZO STERN
CORTE DUCA
C. FRUTTAROL
DUCA
C. LUNGA S. BARNABA
MALPAGA
GRANDE
CA' DEL DUCA
RIO D.
S. VIDAL
PALAZZO LOREDAN
RIO F. LOMBAR
C. D. CERCHIERI
PALAZZO LOREDAN
CALLE VITTURI
RIO DO
PALAZZO FALIER
RIO
CHIESA DI S. VIDAL
EX CONVENTO D. EREMITE
C. EREMITE
TOLETTA
D.
PALAZZO CONTARINI D. SCRIGNI
PALAZZO GIUSTINIAN-LOLIN
Campiello S. Vidal
PAL PI
FOND. BOLLANI
PALAZZO CAVALLI-FRANCHETTI
C. FORNO
C. DELLA TOLETTA
C. CORFÙ
ACCADEMIA
FOND. D. EREMITE
RIO D. ROMITE
FOND. BORGO
PONTE D. ACCADEMIA
Campo d. Carità
PALAZZO BRANDOLIN
FONDAM. PRIULI
PALAZZO GIUSTINIAN-RECANATI
RIO TERRÀ CARITA
GALLERIE DELL' ACCADEMIA
PALAZZO CONTARINI-DAL ZAFFO
DORSODURO

San Marco, the center of aristocratic Venice, is not limited to its famous square, and the best way to discover it is by walking around its campi. First is Campo San Luca, close to the Rialto, then the more intimate Campo San Fantin and, finally, Campo Santo Stefano and Campo San Vidal, forming the heart of the district. From there it's only a few steps to the Accademia bridge. Dorsoduro, to the south, has exceptional museums bordering the Grand Canal: the Gallerie dell'Accademia, the Guggenheim collection and, overlooked by the Salute, the former sea customs house taken over by the Pinault Foundation.

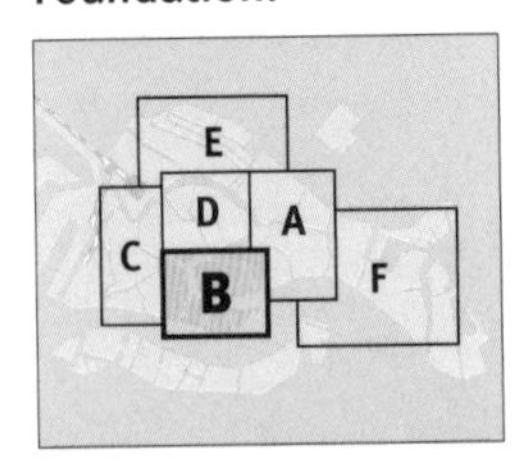

DA FIORE

LINEA D'OMBRA

RESTAURANTS

All' Angolo (**B** D2)
→ *San Marco 3464, Campo Santo Stefano*
Tel. 041 522 07 10
Mon-Sat 7am–9pm
A popular meeting place for the local workforce, with a wide selection of sandwiches, paninis and salads for a light meal at a reasonable price. Small terrace opposite the church of Santo Stefano. Entrées €4–12.

Da Fiore (**B** C1)
→ *San Marco 3461, Calle delle Botteghe*
Tel. 041 523 53 10
Wed-Mon 9.30am–10pm
This Venetian *bacaro* is renowned for its *cicchetti*: *sarde in saor, frittura mista, polpette, seppioline ai ferri* (grilled cuttlefish) and the typical *ombra*. A great place to stop for aperitifs. Don't confuse it with its sister trattoria next door, which isn't nearly as nice. Entrées €5–20.

Zorzi (**B** F1)
→ *San Marco 4359, Calle dei Fuseri*
Tel. 041 520 88 16; Mon-Sat 11.30am–4pm, 4.30–10pm
Good value for money in this authentic osteria, very popular with the locals. Tucked in an 18th-c. palace, the decor is a little kitsch but the Venetian specialties (both meat and fish) are excellent. Prix fixe €15, €20; entrées €9–30.

Bistrot de Venise (**B** F1)
→ *San Marco 4685, Calle dei Fabbri; Tel. 041 523 66 51*
Daily noon–3pm, 7pm–midnight
Service until midnight – something of a rarity in Venice – and a wine bar with three types of cuisine; traditional, creative and the almost forgotten 'Renaissance Venetian'. Entrées €18–34.

Ai Gondolieri (**B** C3)
→ *Dorsoduro 366, Fondamenta Ospedaleto*
Tel. 041 528 63 96; Wed-Mon noon–3pm, 7–10pm
Unusually for Venice, this restaurant only has meat on the menu, served with flavorsome seasonal vegetables. Elegant surroundings and impeccable service. Entrées €20–32.

Linea d'Ombra (**B** E4)
→ *Dorsoduro 19, Fondamenta Zattere ai Saloni; Tel. 041241 18 81*
Daily noon–3pm, 7–10pm (closed Tue in winter)
The elegant, modern setting is mirrored in the sophisticated and inventive cooking,

SEGALIN

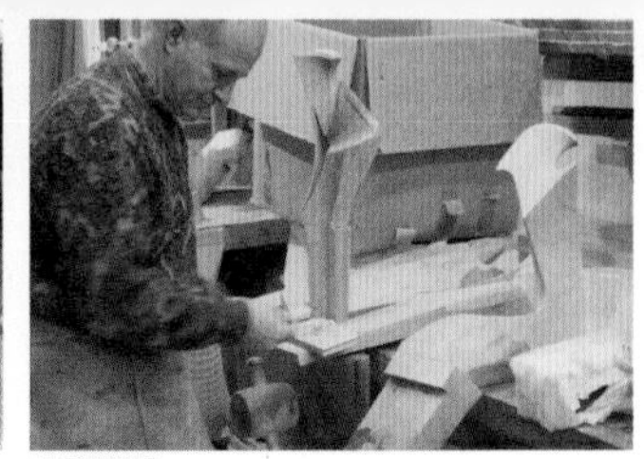

LE FORCOLE

with the emphasis on seafood: lobster and asparagus ravioli; tuna *au gratin* with basil. There are also a few meat dishes, as well as a superb wine list. Delightful terrace overlooking Giudecca Island. Entrées €18–35.

CAFÉS, ICE-CREAM PARLORS, BAR

Gelati Nico (**B** A4)
→ *Dorsoduro 922, Fondamenta Zattere ai Gesuiti; Tel 041 522 52 93; May-Sep: daily 6.45am (7.30am Sun)–11.30pm; Oct-April: Fri-Wed 6.45am (7.30am Sun)– 8.30pm*
Ideally situated in the middle of the peaceful Zattere, this kiosk is renowned among Venetian ice-cream lovers. Don't miss out on the *gianduiotto* (chocolate, nuts and whipped cream).

Lo Squero (**B** A3)
→ *Dorsoduro 990, Fondamenta Nani; Tel 347 269 79 21; Daily 9am–12.30am (9pm in winter)*
The fame of Simone Sambo's luscious Sicilian pistachio ice cream, homemade and super-smooth, has spread as far as Hollywood.

Da Gino (**B** C3)
→ *Dorsoduro 853/A, Calle Sant'Agnese; Tel 041 528 52 76; Mon-Sat 6am–7.30pm*
A very pleasant and friendly neighborhood café, mainly patronized by senior card-players and students of the nearby School of Fine Arts.

Al Volto (**B** E1)
→ *San Marco 4081, Calle Cavalli; Tel. 041 522 89 45 Daily 10am–4pm, 6–10pm*
In a quiet backstreet, an enoteca whose ceiling is plastered with Italian wine-bottle labels. Various *cicchetti* are on offer, along with draught beer and wine.

Paolin (**B** C2)
→ *San Marco 2962, Campo Santo Stefano Tel. 041 522 55 76 Feb-Oct: daily 9am–7.30pm*
This café/ice-cream parlor has a charming terrace on the Campo Santo Stefano – and serve one of the best cappuccinos in town.

SHOPPING

Segalin (**B** F1)
→ *San Marco 4365, Calle dei Fuseri; Tel. 041 522 21 15 Mon-Fri 10am–1pm, 3.30–7pm; Sat 10am–1pm*
In this workshop, which first opened in 1932, Daniela Ghezzo creates the most extravagant shoes in Venice.

Zacaria's (**B** E2)
→ *San Marco 1920, Calle della Fenice Tel. 041 521 13 29 Daily 9.30am–6.30pm (closed Sun in winter)*
Original, colorful collages made with ribbons, textiles and Mondano pearls, depicting carnival characters, gondolas and Venetian palaces. Also, handbags and stationery.

Il Prato (**B** E2)
→ *San Marco 2456/9, Calle delle Ostreghe; Tel 041 523 11 48; Mon-Sat 10am–7.30pm; Sun 11am–7pm*
Handmade paper and notebooks but best of all, beautiful objects made from Murano glass by master craftsmen such as Vivarini, Nason Moretti and others.

Alberto Valese-Ebrû (**B** D2)
→ *San Marco 3471, Campo Santo Stefano; Tel. 041 523 88 30; Mon-Sat 10am–1pm, 2.30–7pm; Sun 11am–6pm*
In his workshop, Alberto Valese creates beautiful marbled paper, on sale by the sheet or crafted into notebooks, bookmarks, pencils, etc.; also natural silk, painted or printed.

Chiarastella Cattana (**B** C1)
→ *San Marco 3357, Salizzada San Samuele Tel. 041 522 43 69; Mon-Sat 10am–1pm, 2.30–7pm (Sat afternoon by appt)*
Quality linen: thick cloths, colored and finely striped, embroidered cushions in pastel hues, and more. Elegance for any budget.

Livio De Marchi (**B** C1)
→ *San Marco 3157/A, Salizzada San Samuele Tel. 041 528 56 94 Mon-Fri 9am–12.30pm, 1.30–4pm (opening hours are variable)*
Leather gloves, an umbrella, a giant tube of paint, a travel bag – all sculpted out of wood in a hyperreal style that brings them to life.

Le Forcole (**B** D4)
→ *Dorsoduro 341, Fondamenta Soranzo della Fornace Tel. 041 522 56 99; Mon-Fri 8.30am–12.30pm, 2–6pm*
A *forcola* is an intricately carved piece of wood that supports the oar on a gondola. Saverio Pastor is one of the last practitioners of this typically Venetian art. Visitors can watch him at work and buy a *forcola* or an explanatory book.

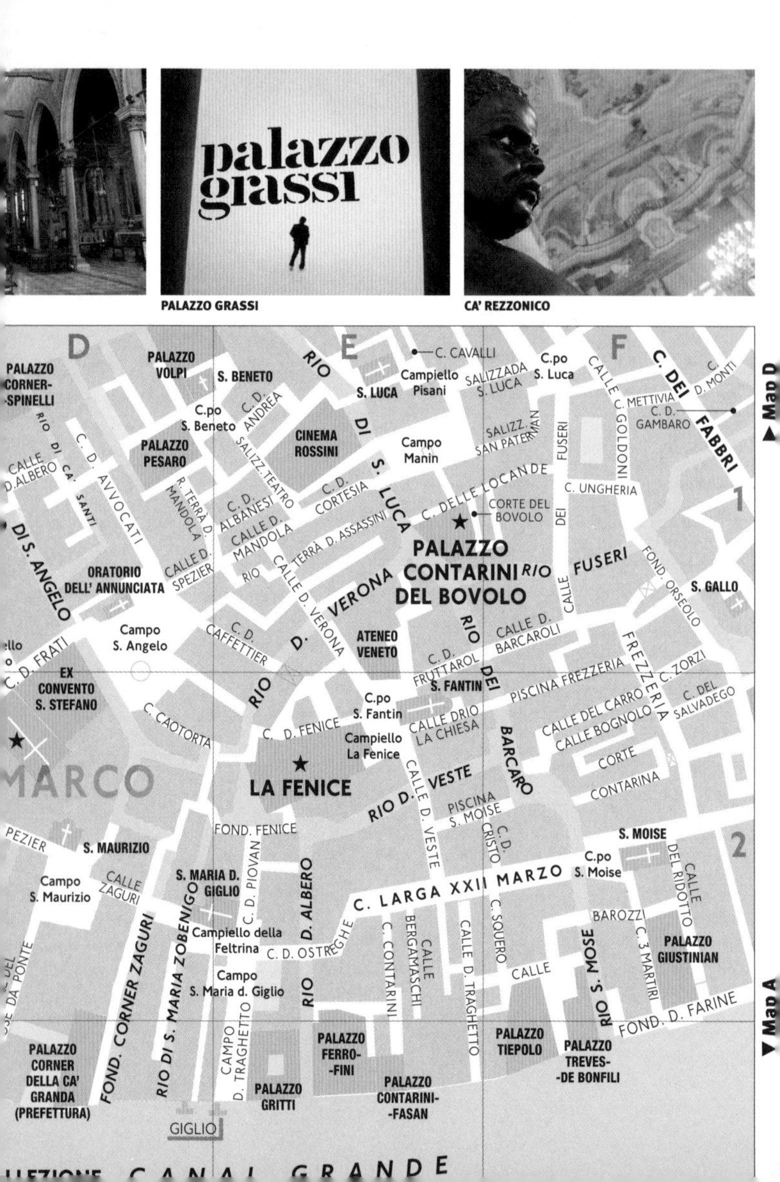
palazzo grassi
PALAZZO GRASSI
CA' REZZONICO
D
E
F
1
2
PALAZZO CORNER-SPINELLI
PALAZZO VOLPI
S. BENETO
C.po S. Beneto
PALAZZO PESARO
CINEMA ROSSINI
S. LUCA
Campiello Pisani
C. CAVALLI
SALIZZADA S. LUCA
C.po S. Luca
C. DEI FABBRI
C. D. MONTI
C. METTIVIA
C. D. GAMBARO
Map D
Campo Manin
SALIZZ. SAN PATERNIAN
FUSERI
C. GOLDONI
C. UNGHERIA
C. DELLE LOCANDE
CORTE DEL BOVOLO
PALAZZO CONTARINI DEL BOVOLO
RIO DI S. LUCA
RIO FUSERI
S. GALLO
FOND. ORSEOLO
ORATORIO DELL' ANNUNCIATA
DI S. ANGELO
Campo S. Angelo
C. D. FRATI
EX CONVENTO S. STEFANO
ATENEO VENETO
S. FANTIN
C.po S. Fantin
Campiello La Fenice
LA FENICE
RIO D. VESTE
C. D. FENICE
C. CAOTORTA
MARCO
FREZZERIA
PISCINA FREZZERIA
CALLE DEL CARRO
CALLE BOGNOLO
CORTE CONTARINA
BARCARO
S. MOISE
C.po S. Moise
C. LARGA XXII MARZO
S. MAURIZIO
Campo S. Maurizio
S. MARIA D. GIGLIO
Campiello della Feltrina
Campo S. Maria d. Giglio
FOND. CORNER ZAGURI
RIO DI S. MARIA ZOBENIGO
PALAZZO CORNER DELLA CA' GRANDA (PREFETTURA)
PALAZZO GRITTI
PALAZZO FERRO-FINI
PALAZZO CONTARINI-FASAN
PALAZZO TIEPOLO
PALAZZO TREVES-DE BONFILI
PALAZZO GIUSTINIAN
RIO S. MOSE
FOND. D. FARINE
Map A
GIGLIO
CANAL GRANDE

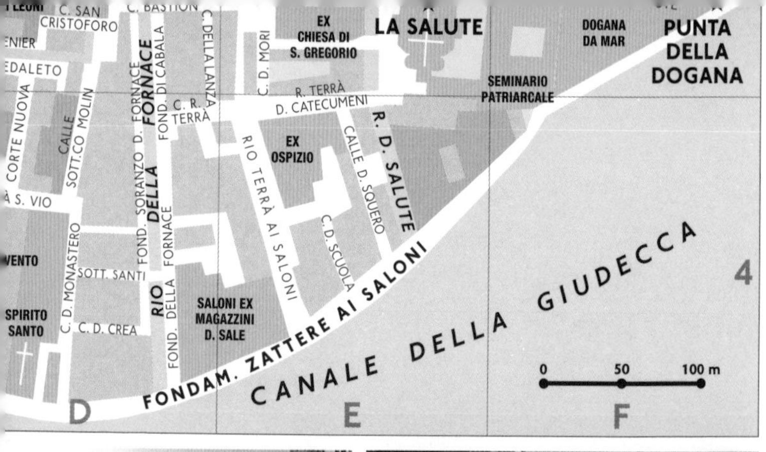

TE

PUNTA DELLA DOGANA

8th century. Richly ted with frescos . Tiepolo (*Nuptial* room), it is a n of decorative m the Venetian nto with glasswork, in, furniture and es. One room is ed to work by Pietro (1702–85), another ait artist Rosalba (1675–1757).

rie cademia (B B3)
duro 1050, ella Carità 22 22 47; Daily 7.15pm (2pm Mon)
onal collection of n paintings from the 14th to the 18th centuries, from Paolo Veneziano (*c.*1290–1360) to Tiepolo via Bellini, Mantegna, Lotto and Tintoretto. Founded in 1807, the gallery was also used by students of the Academy of Fine Arts.

★ I Gesuati (B B4)
→ *Dorsoduro 909, Fondamenta Zattere ai Gesuati; Mon-Sat 10am–5pm*
One of the loveliest rococo interiors in Venice, with four stunning ceiling frescos (1737–39) by G. B. Tiepolo. The Dominicans – not the Jesuits – are responsible for this church (1724–36) and its Palladian-inspired façade.

★ Collezione Peggy Guggenheim (B D3)
→ *Dorsoduro 704, Calle San Cristoforo; Tel. 041 240 54 11; Wed-Mon 10am–6pm*
An important modern art collection assembled by Peggy Guggenheim in the unfinished Palazzo Venier, where she lived for 30 years. Works by Dalí, Calder, Kandinsky, Bacon, Pollock.

★ La Salute (B E3)
→ *Dorsoduro 1, Campo della Salute; Tel. 041 274 39 28 Daily 9am–noon, 3–6pm*
At the mouth of the Grand Canal stands the most imposing example of Venetian Baroque (1631–87, B. Longhena), built to mark the end of the plague epidemic. Ornate façade with 125 statues and an interior rich in paintings by Titian, Tintoretto and Palma the Younger.

★ Punta della Dogana (B F3)
→ *Dorsoduro 2, Campo della Salute; Tel. 199 112 112 Wed-Mon 10am–7pm*
Within the gigantic warehouse of the Punta della Dogana, this addition to the Pinault Foundation was inaugurated in 2009. Contemporary artists include Cy Twombly, Cindy Sherman and Jeff Koons.

CAMPO SAN BARNABA

CHIESA DI SAN TROVASO

★ **Chiesa di San Pantalon** (**C** D3)
→ *Dorsoduro, Campo San Pantalon; Tel. 041 523 58 93*
Mon-Sat 10am–noon, 1–3pm
It took 24 years (1680–1704) for Gian Antonio Fumiani to complete this stunning trompe-l'oeil ceiling. This is one of the largest canvas paintings in the world (1,450 sq. ft), with 40 panels depicting the martyrdom of St Pantaleon.

★ **Scuola Grande dei Carmini** (**C** C4)
→ *Dorsoduro 2617, Santa Margherita; Tel. 041 528 94 20; Daily 11am–5pm*
The fame of this Carmelite scuola is down to the superb ceiling painted by Giambattista Tiepolo between 1739 and 1743. At the center, Our Lady of Carmel, and around her, biblical scenes.

★ **Chiesa dei Carmini** (**C** C5)
→ *Dorsoduro, Campo dei Carmini; Tel. 041 522 65 53*
Variable hours
With a Renaissance façade, baroque-style decor in the nave and Gothic elements in the choir. See the series of paintings depicting the Carmelites' history and an altarpiece of *St Nicholas in Glory Between John the Baptist and St Lucia* (1529) by Lorenzo Lotto, with a realistic landscape.

★ **Campo San Barnaba** (**C** D5)
The campo, a much visited rectangle demarcated by the church at one end and the *rio* (canal) at the other, is a typical layout for the oldest of the campi. The 11th-century bell tower has an unusual conical spire added in the 14th century. Close by is the Ponte dei Pugni, where, until the 18th century, the Castellani and the Nicolotti (rival clans) would meet to fist-fight, egged on by crowds of onlookers. Sculpted footprints show the position of the fighters. There is also a morni floating market.

★ **Chiesa di San Trovaso** (**C** D
→ *Dorsoduro 1098, Campo San Trovaso*
Tel. 041 522 21 33
Mon-Sat 8–11am, 2.30–5.30pm
The church bears tw identical, classical fa – as the joint parish enemy clans, two en were essential. Insic for a fine Renaissan relief (*Angels Bearing Symbols of Christ's Pa St Chrysogonus Moun on a Horse* by Giamb (15th c.) and canvas Tintoretto.

CHIESA DI SAN PANTALON

SCUOLA GRANDE DEI CARMINI

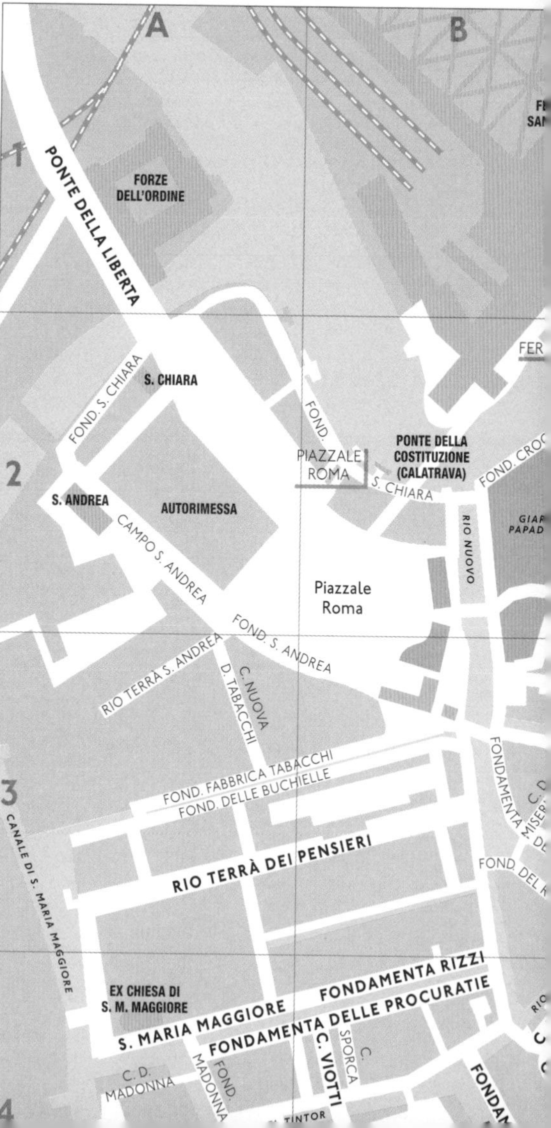

A
B
1
2
3
4
PONTE DELLA LIBERTA
FORZE DELL'ORDINE
S. CHIARA
FOND. S. CHIARA
S. ANDREA
AUTORIMESSA
CAMPO S. ANDREA
FOND.
PIAZZALE ROMA
PONTE DELLA COSTITUZIONE (CALATRAVA)
S. CHIARA
FOND. CROC
RIO NUOVO
Piazzale Roma
FOND. S. ANDREA
RIO TERRÀ S. ANDREA
C. NUOVA D. TABACCHI
FOND. FABBRICA TABACCHI
FOND. DELLE BUCHIELLE
CANALE DI S. MARIA MAGGIORE
RIO TERRÀ DEI PENSIERI
FONDAMENTA C. D. MISER.
FOND. DEL
EX CHIESA DI S. M. MAGGIORE
FONDAMENTA RIZZI
FONDAMENTA DELLE PROCURATIE
S. MARIA MAGGIORE
C. D. MADONNA
FOND. MADONNA
C. VIOTTI
C. SPORCA
FONDAM
TINTOR
FER
GIAR PAPAD
FI SAI

Dorsoduro is one of the largest and most diverse districts of Venice: Campo Santa Margherita, where most bars are open until 2am, is Venice's late-night playground; and Campo San Barnaba, with its numerous shops, stands in stark contrast to the peaceful Briati quay. Heading south, the wide quaysides of the Zattere offer some of the most wonderful walks in the city, with Giudecca Island in the distance. To the north, at the city's gates, the controversial bridge built by the Spanish architect Santiago Calatrava, links the Santa Lucia train station to the Piazzale Roma coach station.

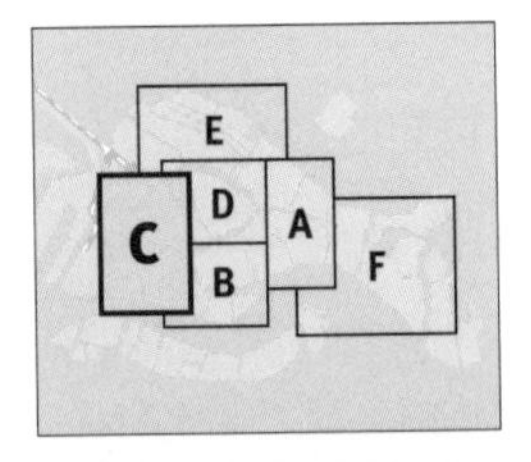

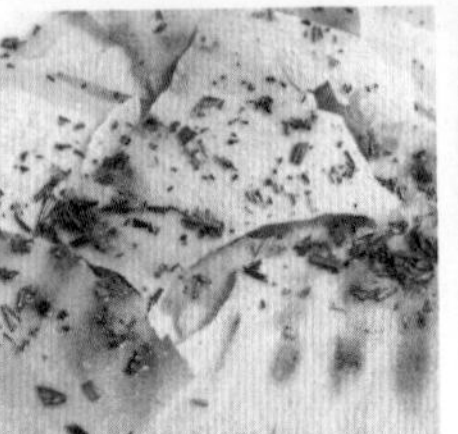

L'INCONTRO

ONIGA

RESTAURANTS

Osteria Alla Bifora (**C** C4)
→ *Dorsoduro 2930, Campo Santa Margherita*
Tel. 041 523 61 19
Daily noon–3pm, 5pm–1am
A picturesque osteria offering smoked-fish carpaccio, *sarde in saor* (marinated sardines), a wide-ranging cheeseboard and copious platters of cold meats. Terrace on the *campo*. Assorted *cicchetti* €20; entrées €6–15.

Al Vecio Marangon (**C** D5)
→ *Dorsoduro Calle della Toletta; Tel. 041 523 57 68*
Daily noon–2pm, 6–10.30pm
Hidden in a back alley, this tiny restaurant has soft lighting, candles on the terrace, attentive service and delicious dishes from all over Italy; fine house wine. Entrées €9–15.

Estro (**C** D3)
→ *Dorsoduro 3778, Crosera San Pantalon*
Tel. 041 476 49 14
Wed-Mon 11am–midnight
Exposed beams and wine racks on the walls in this stylish spot, popular with students from the nearby university. To eat: garnished *focaccia*, lasagne, beef tartare. Extensive wine list. Entrées €10–16.

La Bitta (**C** C5)
→ *Dorsoduro 2753/A, Calle Lunga San Barnaba*
Tel. 041 523 05 31
Mon-Sat 7–11pm
Meat dishes are the main fayre on offer here: jugged rabbit, braised beef, Venetian-style liver; also pasta dishes and a good wine list. Entrées €10–27.

Osteria ai Artisti (**C** D5)
→ *Dorsoduro 1169/A, Fondamenta della Toletta*
Tel. 041 523 89 44; Mon-Sat noon–4pm, 7–10pm
The romantic setting, with candles and a few tables alongside a canal, is perfectly matched by the sophisticated food, based on seasonal ingredients. Entrées €10–35.

L'Incontro (**C** C4)
→ *Dorsoduro 3062/A, Rio Terrà Canal*
Tel. 041 522 24 04
March-Oct: daily 12.30–3pm, 7.30–11pm (closed Mon in winter)
The interior may not be anything special but the traditional Sardinian dishes on offer are truly outstanding, particularly the roast suckling pig

D

IL CAFFÈ ROSSO

ANNELIE PIZZI E RICAMI

(subject to availability). Charming terrace. Entrées €12–28.

Oniga (**C** D5)
→ *Dorsoduro 2852, Campo San Barnaba*
Tel. 041 522 44 10
Wed-Mon noon–3pm, 7–11pm
The copper pans hanging from the ceiling give this restaurant a homely feel. Local specialties with an imaginative twist, as in the red slipper-lobster tagliatelle. Entrées €15–20.

PATISSERIE, CAFÉS, BARS

Tonolo (**C** D3)
→ *Dorsoduro 3764, Calle San Pantalon*
Tel. 041 523 72 09; Tue-Sun 7.45am–8pm (1pm Sun)
This famous patisserie is often packed with locals propped against the bar with a coffee and cake. In the carnival season, sample the *frittelle*, delicious doughnuts sprinkled with sugar.

El Chioschetto (**C** C6)
→ *Dorsoduro 1406, Fondamenta Zattere Ponte Longo; Tel 348 396 84 66*
Daily 8.30am–1am (5pm Oct-Feb; 9pm March-April)
A tiny kiosk with a large terrace facing Giudecca Island, a favorite meeting place for students. Ideal for enjoying the morning sun by the waterside, or for whiling away the evening with a drink and a few *cicchetti*.

Al Bottegon (**C** D6)
→ *Dorsoduro 992, Fondamenta Nani*
Tel. 041 523 00 34
Mon-Sat 8am–8pm
This *cicchetteria*, set alongside a canal directly opposite a delightful stone bridge, is known popularly as '*Gia Schiavi*'. Venetians come here from far and wide to enjoy a drink and savor the huge panini.

Il Caffè Rosso (**C** C4)
→ *Dorsoduro 2963, Campo Santa Margherita*
Tel. 041 528 79 98
Mon-Sat 7am–1am
Impossible to miss this local institution, which owes its name to its bright-red façade. Inside, the old bar is equally striking, although in the evening customers tend to crowd around the tables on the square; sandwiches also available.

Venice Jazz Club (**C** C5)
→ *Dorsoduro 3102, Fondamenta del Squero, Ponte dei Pugni*
Tel. 041 523 20 56
Bar open from 7pm, concerts from 9pm (days vary)
Hushed atmosphere, small round tables, subdued lighting: a true jazz club, where you can also hear blues, bossa nova, etc.

SHOPPING

Annelie Pizzi e Ricami (**C** C5)
→ *Dorsoduro 2748, Calle Lunga San Barnaba*
Tel. 041 520 32 77
Mon-Sat 9.30am–12.30pm, 4–7.30pm
A quaint boutique owned by a talented seamstress; shirts, nightgowns, lace, linen, silk embroidered purses, pearl-strung bags and a superior selection of *pizzi* (laces).

Bressanello Artstudio (**C** D5)
→ *Dorsoduro 2835/A, Ponte dei Pugni*
Tel. 041 724 10 80
Mon-Sat 10am–7pm
Artful photographs in color or black and white, signed Fabio Bressanello. You can buy them framed or unframed.

Signor Blum (**C** D5)
→ *Dorsoduro 2840, Campo San Barnaba*
Tel. 041 522 63 67
Daily 9.30am–2pm, 3–7.30pm (closed Sun in Jan)
The Rialto Bridge, Venetian palaces, jigsaw puzzles and mobiles, all carved in wood and hand-painted.

Gualti (**C** C4)
→ *Dorsoduro 3111, Rio Terrà Canal*
Tel. 041 520 17 31
Mon-Sat 10am–1pm, 3–7pm
Gualti is a talented craftsman who uses a variety of materials (resin, glass, silk) to create jewelry and accessories in unusual designs.

Ca' Macana (**C** D5)
→ *Dorsoduro 3172, Calle delle Botteghe*
Tel. 041 277 61 42
Daily 10am–7.30pm (6.30pm in winter)
When Mario Belloni started creating masks over 30 years ago he only had one competitor in Venice. This talented artist went on to design many of the masks worn in Stanley Kubrick's movie *Eyes Wide Shut*.

Danghyra (**C** D4)
→ *Dorsoduro 3220, Calle del Capeler*
Tel. 041 522 41 95
Wed-Mon 10am–1pm, 3–7pm
A stunning collection of handmade pottery: brightly colored cups and vases glazed with gold or platinum.

CANAL GRANDE

C

D

1

2

3

4

CHIESA DEGLI SCALZI

FERROVIA

PONTE SCALZI

Campo di S. Simeone Profeta

S. SIMEONE GRANDE

S. SIMEON PICCOLO

CAMPIELLO D. COMARE

C. LUNGA CHIOVERETTE

CORTE PISANI

C. DEL PISTOR

CALLE CORRERA

RIVA DI BIASIO

C. SPORCA

LISTA DEI BARI

R. 5° GALLION

CALLE ZEN

C. PO RIELLO

RIO TERRÀ

SALIZZADA ZUSTO

CALLE ORSETTI

C. DELLE SAVIE

CALLE RUGA VECCHIA

RUGA BELLA

C. DEI SQUARTAI

C. LARGA DEI BARI

C. D. CROCE

FONDAMENTA RIO MARIN

FOND. GRADENIGO

C. GRADISCA

C. VENZATO

CASA CAPPELLO

FOND. RIO MARIN

R. D. CHIOVERETTE

CALLE DEL TRAGHETTO DI LUCIA

C. DEI BERGAMASCHI

CORTE CANAL

C. VISCIGA

C. LARGA CONTARINA

C. S. ZUANE

RAMO D'OCHE

C. CAPPELLO

SANTA CROCE

CAMPO DELLA LANA

CASE NUOVE

SCUOLA DI SAN GIOVANNI EVANGELISTA

STP. D. LACCA

C. DEL CAMPAZZO

CALLE DI MEZZO

SAN POLO

C. ZANE

C. DELLA VIDA

Campo San Stin

RIO SAN TOMA

CALLE AMAI

R. D. MUNEGHETTE

TOLENTINI

C. DELLE CHIOVERE

C. DIETRO L'ARCHIVIO

RAMO S. NICOLETO

RAMO CIMESIN

I FRARI

S. ROCCO

C. TINTORETTO

Campo dei Frari

RIO DELLE SACCHERE

C. FALIER

C. DEL FORNO

SAL. S. PANTALON

CALLE VINANTI

SCUOLA GRANDE DI SAN ROCCO

Campo S. Rocco

C. D. SCUOLA

SAL. S. ROCCO

C. DEI CORTI

Campo S. Toma

MINOTTO

GAFFARO

FOND. GAFFARO

RIO DEL MALCANTON

FOND. MALCANTON

Campiello d. Mosche

RIO DELLE MOSCHE

FOND. D. OMESTA

RIO DELLA FRESCADA

FOND. DEL FORNER

C. DE BASEGO

RIO NUOVO

FOND. DEL RIO NUOVO

CHIESA DI ★ SAN PANTALON

PONTE S. MARGHERITA

Campo San Pantalon

C. S. PANTALON

CROSERA S. PANTALON

CALLE DELLA SAONERIA

C. LARGA FOSCARI

C. DE LA FRESCADA

PALAZZO BALBI

C. D. CAFFETIER

C. DEL FORNO

CORTE D. FONDEGO

RIO FOSCARI

UNIVERSITÀ

SQUERO DI SAN TROVASO

ZATTERE

▶ Map D

▼ Maps B/D

CHIESA DELL'ANGELO RAFFAELE

CHIESA DI SAN NICOLÒ DEI MENDICOLI

ero di San o (**C** D6)
duro 1097, Campo vaso; no visits allowed
uero (boat yard), one ast three remaining a workshops in the n be seen from the de of the canal. ey make, repair, nd varnish the s. The chalet-like gs are reminiscent of the Cadore, an egion where the en originated.

re (**C** C6)
th century the *nte* (broad paved es built in 1516) ding points for lumber, delivered by flotation. The activity provided by the unloading of the rafts (*zattere*) has now been replaced by that of the café terraces.

★ Chiesa di San Sebastiano (**C** B5)
→ *Dorsoduro 1686, Campo San Sebastiano; Mon-Sat 10am–5pm (see Chorus in Practical Venice)*
A series of dazzlingly colored paintings by Veronese is hidden behind this modest façade. On the sacristy ceiling is his *Crowning of the Virgin* (1555), one of the first works he was commissioned to do. Until 1565 Veronese applied his genius to the choir nave, and at his request he was buried in the church.

★ Chiesa di San Nicolò dei Mendicoli (**C** A5)
→ *Dorsoduro 1907, Campo San Nicolò; Tel. 041 275 03 82 Mon-Sat 10am–noon, 3–5.30pm; Sun 10am–noon*
At the far eastern end of Venice, this Romanesque church, rare in its charm and simplicity, has remained unaltered since the 12th century. It owes its survival to the poverty of the area, filled with *mendicoli* (beggars), where rich merchants had no wish to spend or invest money. The layout is a three-nave basilica with a central apse and typical Venetian-Byzantine bell tower. See the wooden statues and iconostasis.

★ Chiesa dell'Angelo Raffaele (**C** B5)
→ *Dorsoduro, Campo dell' Angelo Raffaele; Tel. 041 522 85 48; Mon-Sat 10am–noon, 3–5.30pm; Sun 9am–noon*
Another masterpiece, this one by the uncontested master of Venetian rococo, Gianantonio Guardi (1699–1760). Beneath the high ceiling are five panels depicting, in extraordinary radiance, the life of the prophet Tobias (1749).

SCUOLA DI SAN GIOVANNI

CHIESA DI SAN GIACOMO DALL'ORIO

CHIESA DI SANTA MARIA MATER DOMINI

★ **Ponte di Rialto/ Rialto Bridge** (**D** F3)
The first of Venice's stone constructions (1591) to span the Grand Canal and, until the 19th century, the only link between the two banks. The ambitious project presented by the aptly named Antonio Da Ponte was chosen over those of Sansovino and Michelangelo. There are 6,000 pilings for one single arch (25 ft in height), allowing galley ships to pass under it.

★ **Mercati di Rialto** (**D** E3)
→ *San Polo, Fabbriche Nuove and Campo Beccarie; Tue-Sat 7am–1pm; Campo de la Pescheria (fish market): Tue-Sat 7am–12.30pm*
Formerly the social and economic heart of the city, where goods from the East and the West were traded, the Rialto markets remain one of the busiest areas in Venice. The gold and spices may have gone, but trading activity is still intense and colorful.

★ **Ca' Goldoni** (**D** B4)
→ *San Polo 2794, Palazzo Centani; Tel. 041 275 93 25 Thu-Tue 10am–5pm (4pm in winter)*
This typical Gothic palace (15th c.), the birthplace of the famous playwright Carlo Goldoni (1707–93), is now a modest theater museum housing 18th-century collections (puppet theater, portraits, original manuscripts, etc.). Access is via the splendid covered staircase, with stone lions adorning the banister.

★ **Scuola Grande di San Rocco** (**D** A4)
→ *San Polo 3052, Campo San Rocco; Tel. 041 523 48 64 Daily 9.30am–5.30pm*
Enriched by donations, this scuola patronized Tintoretto for 23 years, during which time he decorated it with 56 paintings, including his *Crucifixion* (1565), one of the most beautiful sacred paintings of the Vene School.

★ **Chiesa di Santa Gloriosa dei Frari**
→ *San Polo 3072, Cam dei Frari; Tel. 041 275 0 Daily 9am (1pm Sun)–*
The largest church in Venice (1340–1443), has an unusual brick façade punctuated w marble ornaments. T Canova and some of city's doges are buri here. The stunning G basilica has carved wooden choir stalls Cozzi, and canvases Giovanni Bellini and (*Madonna di Ca' Pesc* and *Assumption*).

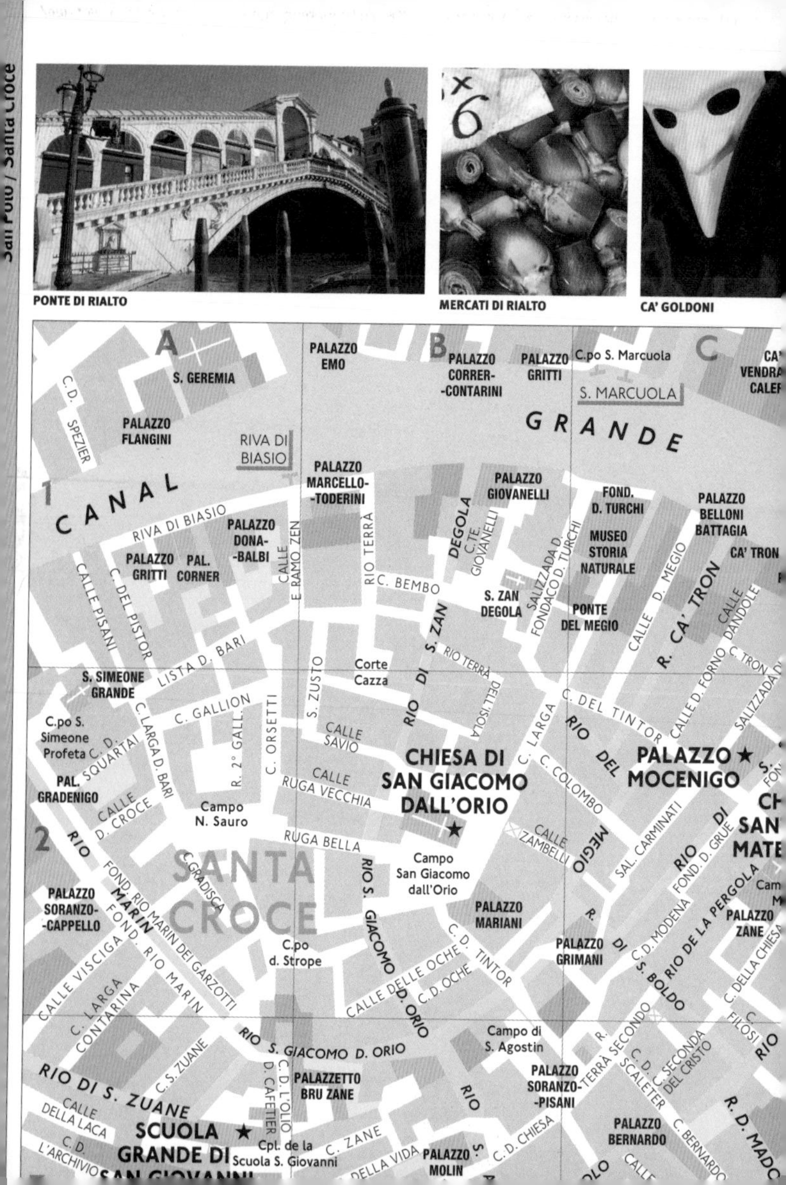

PONTE DI RIALTO
MERCATI DI RIALTO
CA' GOLDONI
A
B
C
1
2
S. GEREMIA
PALAZZO EMO
PALAZZO CORRER-CONTARINI
PALAZZO GRITTI
C.po S. Marcuola
S. MARCUOLA
C.D. SPEZIER
PALAZZO FLANGINI
RIVA DI BIASIO
CANAL GRANDE
PALAZZO MARCELLO-TODERINI
PALAZZO GIOVANELLI
FOND. D. TURCHI
PALAZZO BELLONI BATTAGIA
RIVA DI BIASIO
PALAZZO DONA-BALBI
PALAZZO GRITTI
PAL. CORNER
CALLE E RAMO ZEN
RIO TERRÀ
DEGOLA
C.TE. GIOVANELLI
SALIZZADA D. FONDACO D. TURCHI
MUSEO STORIA NATURALE
CA' TRON
CALLE PISANI
C. DEL PISTOR
C. BEMBO
S. ZAN DEGOLA
PONTE DEL MEGIO
CALLE D. MEGIO
R. CA' TRON
CALLE DANDOLE
LISTA D. BARI
RIO DI S. ZAN
RIO TERRÀ DELL'ISOLA
S. ZUSTO
Corte Cazza
CALLE D. FORNO
C. TRON
SALIZZADA
S. SIMEONE GRANDE
C. GALLION
C. ORSETTI
C. LARGA
C. DEL TINTOR
RIO DEL
C.po S. Simeone Profeta
C. D. SQUARTAI
C. LARGA D. BARI
R. 2° GALL.
CALLE SAVIO
CALLE RUGA VECCHIA
CHIESA DI SAN GIACOMO DALL'ORIO
C. COLOMBO
PALAZZO MOCENIGO
PAL. GRADENIGO
CALLE D. CROCE
Campo N. Sauro
RUGA BELLA
CALLE ZAMBELLI
MEGIO
SAL. CARMINATI
RIO DI
SAN MATE
RIO
FOND. RIO MARIN
C. GRADISCA
SANTA CROCE
RIO S. GIACOMO
Campo San Giacomo dall'Orio
FOND. D. GRUE
PALAZZO SORANZO-CAPPELLO
MARIN
FOND. RIO MARIN DEI GARZOTTI
PALAZZO MARIANI
R. DI S. BOLDO
C. D. MODENA
RIO DE LA PERGOLA
PALAZZO ZANE
C.po d. Strope
C. D. TINTOR
PALAZZO GRIMANI
C. DELLA CHIESA
CALLE VISCIGA
FOND. RIO MARIN
C. LARGA CONTARINA
CALLE DELLE OCHE
C. D. OCHE
D. ORIO
C. FILOSI
Campo di S. Agostin
R. TERRÀ SECONDO
C. D. SCALETER
C. SECONDA DEL CRISTO
RIO
RIO DI S. ZUANE
C.S. ZUANE
RIO S. GIACOMO D. ORIO
C. D. L'OLIO
D. CAFETIER
PALAZZETTO BRU ZANE
PALAZZO SORANZO-PISANI
RIO
R. D. MADO
CALLE DELLA LACA
SCUOLA GRANDE DI SAN GIOVANNI
C. D. L'ARCHIVIO
Cpl. de la Scuola S. Giovanni
C. ZANE
DELLA VIDA
PALAZZO MOLIN
C. D. CHIESA
PALAZZO BERNARDO
C. BERNARDO

At the meeting point of San Marco to the east, San Polo to the west and Cannaregio to the north, the Rialto has been vibrating to the rhythm of Venetian merchant life since the 9th century. Apart from the traghetti that come and go across the Grand Canal, its famous bridge linking the three neighboring sestieri is the only way to cross the canal. Two steps away from its archways is the Rialto market that buzzes all morning and, surrounding it, some of the finest palaces and religious buildings in the city. For a calmer tempo, head west away from the crowd to peaceful Santa Croce, with its fine restaurants and discreet terraces.

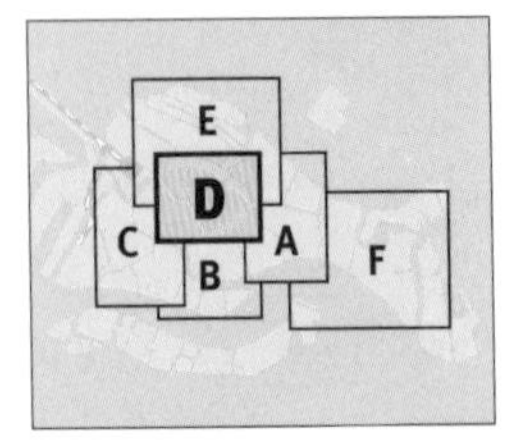

LA ZUCCA

ANTICHE CARAMPANE

RESTAURANTS

Acqua e Mais (**D** D3)
→ *San Polo 1411, Campiello dei Meloni; Tel. 041 296 05 30; Summer: daily 9.30am–8.30pm; Winter: Tue-Sun 9.30am–7.30pm*
Fish and chips Venetian style! Paper cones crammed with grilled or fried fish, as well as polenta and vegetables. The fresh, high-quality ingredients and low prices have earned this modest place great popularity. Take out only. €3.50–5.50.

Al Nono Risorto (**D** D2)
→ *Santa Croce 2338, Sotoportego de Siora Bettina; Tel. 041 524 11 69 Thu-Tue noon–2.30pm, 7–11pm (closed Thu noon–2.30pm in winter)*
The reputation of this restaurant was built on its pizzas and the variety of its dishes, which include *baccalà* (cod) *alla vicentina* and cuttlefish with polenta. A bonus is the leafy interior garden. Pizza €6–12; entrées €9–18.

La Zucca (**D** C1)
→ *Santa Croce 1762, Ponte del Megio Tel. 041 524 15 70; Mon-Sat 12.30–2.30pm, 7–10.30pm*
Try the cozy La Zucca for something a little different: pumpkin and ricotta flan, leek fondue with gorgonzola and stuffed mushrooms. Entrées €9–20.

Naranzaria (**D** F3)
→ *San Polo 130, Campo San Giacometto; Tel 041 724 10 35; Daily 12.30–3pm, 7.30–10.30pm (closed Mon Feb-Easter)*
The chef, a pro with raw fish, successfully mixes Japanese and Italian flavors: sushi, smoked swordfish carpaccio, sesame *yakitori*. The terrace overlooks the Grand Canal. Entrées €14–21.

Antiche Carampane (**D** D3)
→ *San Polo 1911, Rio Terrà Carampane; Tel. 041 524 01 65; Tue-Sat 12.45–2.30pm, 7.30–10.30pm*
This highly reputed restaurant is hidden away in a maze of back streets. Sophisticated dishes featuring monkfish and John Dory, as well as exquisite platters of fried fish. Terrace in the summer. Entrées €16–25.

Da Fiore (**D** C3)
→ *San Polo 2202/A, Calle del Scaleter Tel. 041 72 13 08; Tue-Sat 12.30–2pm, 7–10.30pm*
The epitome of Venetian

A DO MORI

EMILIO CECCATO

ANTICA DROGHERIA MASCARI

cuisine and, for many, the pest restaurant in Venice. Chestnut-filled calamari, *canoce*, artichoke and scamorza cheese pie. Reserve. Entrées €25–42.

PATISSERIE, BARS, CE-CREAM PARLOR

Gelateria Alaska (**D** A2)
→ *Santa Croce 1159, Calle Larga dei Bari*
Tel. 041 71 52 11; Daily 1am–11pm (closed Dec-Jan)
Carlo Pistacchi makes his mouthwatering ice reams with classic lavors as well as unusual lternatives (artichoke, inger, carrot, fennel), lways using fresh easonal produce.

Rizzardini (**D** D3)
→ *San Polo 1415, ampiello dei Meloni*
el. 041 522 38 35
Ved-Mon 7am–8pm
his old-fashioned atisserie, with its 1920s' ood paneling and candy rs, is a treat for both the yes and the taste buds. ll the typical Venetian *olci* are on offer, to take way or eat on the spot: cotta cake, strudel and *ori* (outsize almond hortbread cookies).

a Filo (**D** B2)
→ *Santa Croce 1539, Campo an Giacomo dall'Orio*
Tel. 041 524 65 54
Daily 11am–11pm
This neighborhood bar has a relaxed feel, with its recycled furniture, books, games and piano. Enjoy a quiet drink on the terrace, far from the crowds.

Cantina Do Mori (**D** E3)
→ *San Polo 429, Calle dei Do Mori (between Calle della Donzella and Calle Drio la Scimia); Tel. 041 522 54 01*
Mon-Sat 8.30am–8pm
The oldest *bacaro* in Venice (1462), the 'Moors' Cellar' oozes history. Lots of *tramezzini*, *vassoio misto* (selection of various dishes) and over 100 wines. No tables but a few benches and some barrels to lean against.

All'Arco (**D** E3)
→ *San Polo 436, Calle dell Occhialer; Tel. 041 520 56 66; April-Nov: Mon-Fri 8am–2.30pm (8.30pm Wed-Fri); Dec-March: Mon-Sat 8am–2.30pm*
A favorite bar of the shopkeepers on the Rialto, with a dizzying choice of *cicchetti* and varieties of wine; small terrace outside.

Caffè dei Frari (**D** B3)
→ *San Polo 2564, Fondamenta dei Frari*
Tel. 041 524 18 77
Daily 8.30am–9.30pm (5.30pm Sun)
This two-story café, one of the oldest in town (1870), holds a strategic position across from the Chiesa dei Frari.

SHOPPING

Emilio Ceccato (**D** F3)
→ *San Polo 16, Ponte di Rialto; Tel. 041 522 27 00*
Daily 10am (11am Sun)–1.30pm, 2.30–7pm
Before surrendering to the call of the gondoliers, you can buy their striped shirts and scarves in this shop, which supplies all trades.

Antica Drogheria Mascari (**D** E3)
→ *San Polo 381, Ruga del Spezier; Tel. 041 522 97 62; Mon-Sat 8am–1pm, 4–7.30pm*
A grocery store crammed with teas, spices, candies, dried fruit, nuts, oils, vinegars and jams – and, at the back, one of the best stocked wine cellars in town.

Monica Daniele (**D** C3)
→ *San Polo 2235, Calle del Scaleter*
Tel. 041 524 62 42
Mon-Sat 9am–12.30pm, 2.30–6pm; Sun 9am–1pm
This shop, set in an old *bottega* that once counted Casanova among its customers, now sells Monica Daniele's striking hats and *tabarri* (traditional long black capes).

Paper Owl (**D** C3)
→ *Santa Croce 2155/A, Calle Seconda del Cristo*
Tel. 041 476 19 74
Mon-Sat 8am–6pm (closed Sat in winter)
Exquisite pieces made with paper by Stefania Giannici in this workshop-store: mobiles, jewelry, flowers, boxes and picture frames.

VizioVirtù (**D** B4)
→ *San Polo 2898/A, Calle del Campaniel*
Tel. 041 275 01 49
Daily 10am–7.30pm (closed Sun June-Aug)
Chocolate in an array of imaginative configurations: as a coating for crystallized orange slices or sugared kiwi fruit, as well as fondues and cups of thick hot chocolate.

Il Baule Blù (**D** B4)
→ *San Polo 2916/A, Calle Seconda del Cristo*
Tel. 041 71 94 48
Mon-Sat 10.30am–12.30pm, 4–7pm
A workshop for repairing old toys, combined with a thrift store selling toys from the past such as tin soldiers, record players and teddy bears.

GRANDE DI SAN ROCCO

CHIESA DI SANTA MARIA GLORIOSA DEI FRARI

D
E
F
PALAZZO PAPAFAVA
0
20
100 m
MARIA
OALENA
PAL.
CORRER-
-CONTARINI
VIA V. EMANUELE
S. FOSCA
PALAZZO
GIOVANELLI
NOALE
FOND. S. FELICE
C. D. RACCHETTA
CANNAREGIO
RIO
FOND.
SANT'ANDREA
DE S. ANDREA
C. DELL'OLIO
C. D. FIORI
PALAZZO
MOLIN
DI
C. D. STUA
FOND. D. CHIESA
S. FELICE
CALLE LARGA
DOGE PRIULI
RIO
C. CORRENTE
C. D. ALBANESI
R. ALBANESI
DUE POZZI
R. DI CA' DOLCE
1
PALAZZO
GUSSONI-
-GRIMANI
RIO
Campo
S. Felice
S. FELICE
DI
C. S. FELICE
C. D. PISTOR
C. DEL FORNO
CALLE ZOTTI
CALLE D. VELE
RUGA
PRIULI
PALAZZO
BOLDU
RIO
STRADA
RAMO CA' D'ORO
C. PRIULI
RIO TERRÀ
D. FRANCESCHI
CA' PESARO
GALL. ARTE
MODERNA
PALAZZO
FONTANA
CALLE CA' D'ORO
NOVA
S. SOFIA
C. D. FORNO
CALLE D. VERDE
C. D. MADONNA
SALIZZ. D. PISTOR
C. D. OCA
D. DE
CA' PESARO
TORRI
CA' CORNER
D. REGINA
C. D. REGINA
CALLE D. ROSA
CA' D'ORO
CA'D'ORO
PALAZZO
SAGREDO
D. RAVANO
S. CASSAN
PALAZZO
BRANDOLIN
PALAZZO
FOSCARI
PALAZZO
MICHIEL
D. COLONNE
SS. APOSTOLI
C.po dei
Ss. Apostoli
2
REGINA
C. DEL CAMPANILE
FOND. D. OGIO
PESCHERIA
SCU. D. ANGELO
CUSTODE
RIO D.
SANTI
O MORO
S. CASSIANO
C.po
S. Cassan
TOPORTEGO
DE SIORA
BETTINA
C. D. SCRINIA
C. DEI BOTTERI
BECCARIE
C. BECCARIE
C.po della
Pescaria
PALAZZO
FALIER
CA'
DE MASTO
C.po
Riccardo
Selvatico
FABBRICHE
NUOVE
PALAZZO
MUTI-BAGLIONI
C.po
Beccarie
C. 1° D. DONZELLA
CALLE DRIO LA SCIMIA
RUGA DEL SPEZIERI
MERCATI
DI RIALTO
AN POLO
DELLE
C. ANGELO
C. GALEAZZA
C.po
Beccarie
S. GIOVANNI
CRISOSTOMO
C. MODENA
Campiello
d. Sansoni
CALLE S. MATTIO
C. D. OCCHIALER
FABBRICHE
VECCHIE
PALAZZO
MOLIN-
-CAPPELLO
RIO
S. GIACOMO
DI RIALTO
C.po San
Giacometto
C. ASEO
SALIZZ. S. GIOV. CRISOSTOMO
RUGA DEGLI
S. GIOVANNI
ELEMOSINARIO
PALAZZO D.

▶ Map E

▼ Map A

◀ Maps A/D

MOCENIGO

CA' PESARO

sa di San Giacomo io (**D** B2)
Croce, Campo San dall'Orio; Mon-Sat pm (see Chorus al Venice)
rpiece of Venetian tyle. The stunning ceiling dominates , which is shaped ip's keel. Fine s by Lotto, Palma ger and Veronese.

a Grande Giovanni ista (**D** A3)
lo 2454, Campiello la San Giovanni 82 34; visits by appt scuolasangiovanni.it
carved marble portal by Lombardo (1481), two-flight staircase (1498) by Codussi and stunning colored geometric marble flooring in the Sala Capitolare upstairs. This scuola, one of the oldest in Venice (1261), was stripped of its remaining decoration in 1807 following the Napoleonic decree banning the scuole.

★ Chiesa di Santa Maria Mater Domini (**D** C2)
→ Santa Croce 2123, Campo Santa Maria Mater Domini Mon-Sat 10am–noon
Constructed between two existing buildings, as were many of Venice's small churches, the Renaissance-influenced façade (early 16th century) is made from Istrian stone and attributed to Sansovino. Don't miss Tintoretto's *Invention of the Cross*.

★ Ca' Pesaro (**D** D1)
→ Santa Croce 2076, Fondamenta de Ca' Pesaro Tel. 041 72 11 27; Tue-Sun 10am–6pm (5pm Nov-March)
A museum of modern art and one of Europe's major Oriental art collections are housed here, in a palace that is a triumph of Venetian-Baroque design (1679). There are works by Klimt, Klee, Chagall and Kandinsky, and Venetian painters from the late 1800s. Also superb Japanese costumes and textiles from the Edo period (1600–1868).

★ Palazzo Mocenigo (**B** C2)
→ Santa Croce 1992, Salizzada di San Stae; Tel. 041 72 17 98 Tue-Sun 10am–5pm
This 17th-century palace has been converted into a costume museum, with richly attired dummies holding court in ornately decorated rooms to illustrate the lifestyle of 18th-c. Venetian patricians. One section is given over to perfume, with a reconstruction of a workshop.

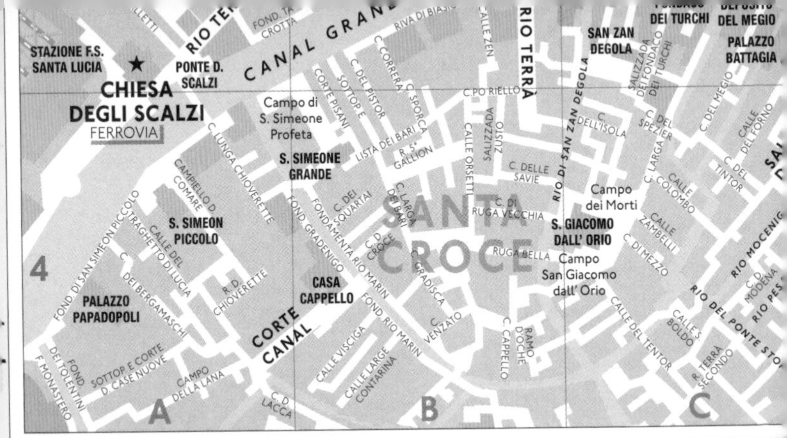

PONTE DEI TRE ARCHI

MUSEO EBRAICO

CHIESA DELLA MADONNA

★ **Chiesa di San Marcuola** (**E** C3)
→ *Cannaregio 1777, Campo San Marcuola; Tel 041 71 38 72; Mon-Sat 9.30am–11am*
The 18th-century unfinished brick façade of this humble church faces a quiet landing stage on the Grand Canal. The altar by Morlaiter contrasts with the plain single nave, which also houses *The Last Supper* (1547) by Tintoretto.

★ **Ca' Vendramin Calergi** (**E** C3)
→ *Cannaregio 2040, Calle Vendramin; Tel. 041 276 04 07 Guided visits by appt: Tue and Sat am, Thu pm. Casino: daily 11.30am–2.30am*
With alternating columns and twin-bay windows, this perfectly balanced façade (16th c.) is often considered to be the finest example of Renaissance architecture in Venice. It was once home to Wagner, who died here on February 13, 1883. Since 1946 the palace has housed the casino.

★ **Ca' d'Oro** (**E** E4)
→ *Cannaregio 3932, Calle Ca' d'Oro; Tel. 041 522 23 49 Mon-Sat 8.15am–7.15pm (2pm Mon); Sun 10am–6pm*
An Oriental influence is clear in this prime example of the city's Flamboyant Gothic style (1440), designed by Bon and Raverti: delicately carved loggias, ogive windows and turrets. In 1916 Baron Franchetti donated this 'House of Gold' to the city, along with his art collection: Venetian- and Tuscan-school paintings, Flemish tapestries, bronze statues.

★ **Chiesa di San Geremia** (**E** B3)
→ *Cannaregio 335, Campo San Geremia; Tel. 041 71 61 81 Mon-Sat 9am–noon, 4.30–6.30pm; Sun 9.30am–12.15pm, 5.30–6.30pm*
Luminous white vaults, baroque altars and paintings by Palma the Younger in this church where the remains of St Lucy have lain since 1860, stole
Constantinople in 10

★ **Chiesa degli Scalzi** (**E** A3)
→ *Cannaregio 54; Tel.*
51 15; Daily 7.30am (7a
Sun)–11.50am, 4–6.40
The majesty of this m
façade contrasted sh
with the poverty of th
barefoot (*scalzi*) Carm
order who lived here
equally ornate baroc
interior (1656) was da
during World War On
that remains of Tiep
work is a single fresc

★ **Chiesa della Ma dell'Orto** (**E** D2)
→ *Cannaregio 3511,*
Fondamenta della Ma

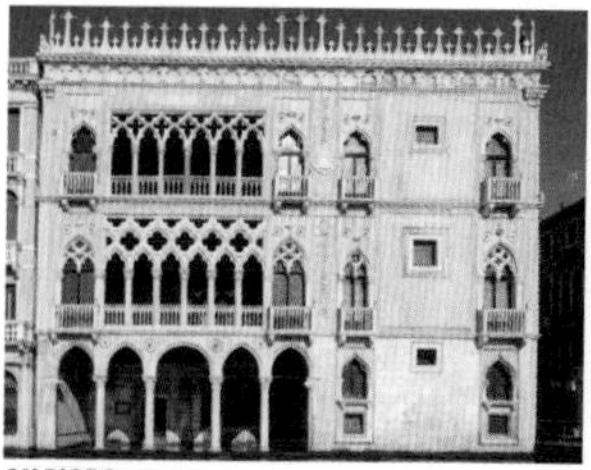
CA' D'ORO

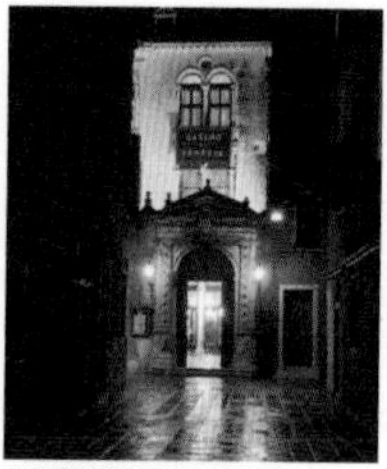
CA' VENDRAMIN CALERGI

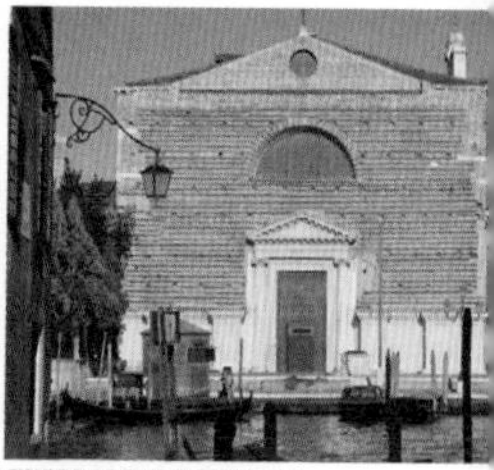
CHIESA DI SAN MARCUOLA

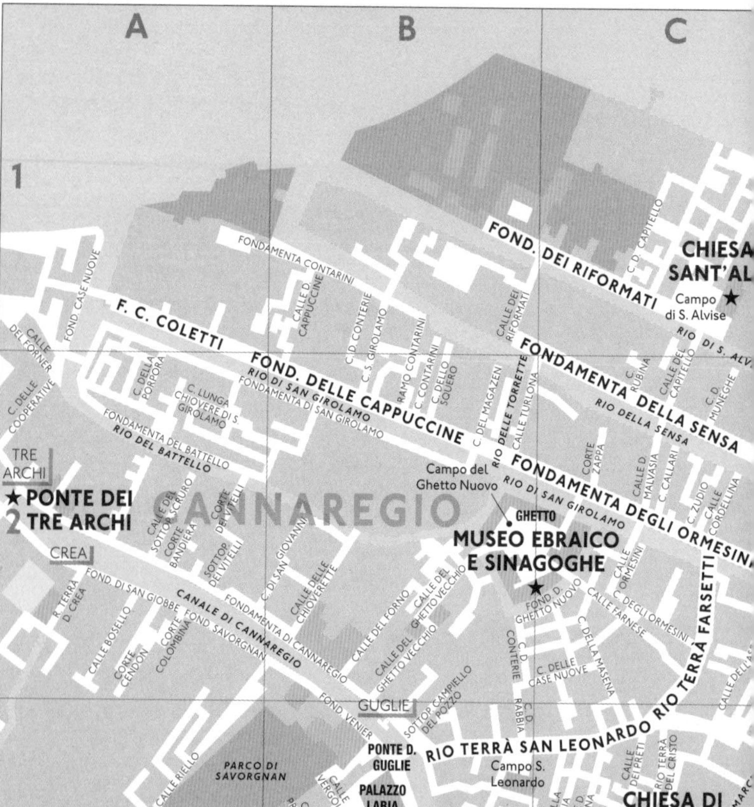
A
B
C
1
2
CANNAREGIO
PONTE DEI TRE ARCHI
TRE ARCHI
CREA
MUSEO EBRAICO E SINAGOGHE
GHETTO
Campo del Ghetto Nuovo
CHIESA SANT'AL
Campo di S. Alvise
CHIESA DI SAN MARCUOLA
PALAZZO LABIA
Campo S. Geremia
PONTE D. GUGLIE
GUGLIE
Campo S. Leonardo
PARCO DI SAVORGNAN
FOND. DEI RIFORMATI
F. C. COLETTI
FOND. DELLE CAPPUCCINE
FONDAMENTA DELLA SENSA
FONDAMENTA DEGLI ORMESINI
RIO TERRÀ FARSETTI
RIO TERRÀ SAN LEONARDO
CANALE DI CANNAREGIO
RIO DI SAN GIROLAMO
RIO DEL BATTELLO
RIO DELLA SENSA
RIO DELLE TORRETTE
RIO DI S. ALVISE
FONDAMENTA CONTARINI
FOND. CASE NUOVE
FONDAMENTA DI SAN GIROLAMO
FONDAMENTA DEL BATTELLO
FONDAMENTA DI CANNAREGIO
FOND. DI SAN GIOBBE
FOND. SAVORGNAN
FOND. VENIER
FOND. D. GHETTO NUOVO
CALLE DEL FORNER
C. DELLE COOPERATIVE
C. DELLA PORPORA
C. LUNGA CHIOVERE DI S. GIROLAMO
CALLE DEL SOTTOP. SCRURO
CORTE BANDIERA
CORTE DEI VITELLI
SOTTOP. DEI VITELLI
C. DI SAN GIOVANNI
CALLE DELLE CHIOVERETTE
CALLE DEL FORNO
CALLE DEL GHETTO VECCHIO
SOTTOP. CAMPIELLO DEL POZZO
CALLE D. CAPPUCCINE
C. D. CONTERIE
C. S. GIROLAMO
RAMO CONTARINI
C. CONTARINI
C. DELLO SQUERO
C. DEL MAGAZEN
CALLE TURLONA
CALLE DEI RIFORMATI
C. D. CAPITELLO
C. RUBINA
CALLE DEL CAPITELLO
C. D. MUNEGHE
CORTE ZAPPA
CALLE D. MALVASIA
C. CALLARI
C. ZUDIO
CALLE CORDELLINA
CALLE ORMESINI
C. DEGLI ORMESINI
CALLE FARNESE
C. DELLA MASENA
C. DELLE CASE NUOVE
C. D. CONTERIE
C. D. RABBIA
CALLE DEI PRETI
RIO TERRÀ DEL CRISTO
C. DELLA PAGLIA
CALLE D. COLONNA
C. E QUERINI
C. EMO
R. TERRÀ D. CREA
CALLE BOSELLO
CORTE CENDON
CORTE COLOMBINA
CALLE RIELLO
CALLE PESARO
CALLE VERGOLA
C. DELLE PROCURATIE

Cannaregio has many personalities. To the north are narrow little streets where the washing lines are strung up like multicolored garlands, Sant' Alvise square, the three-arched bridge quaysides and the old Jewish ghetto – the first in the world and recognizable by its six- to nine-storey dwellings. Here the canals widen and, on the level of the Fondamenta della Misericordia, are lined with bars and restaurants. Eastward, the large quays of the Fondamente Nove look north toward the island of San Michele, whose pink walls enclose Venice's cemetery. Southward, along the Grand Canal, the Strada Nova is abuzz with trade.

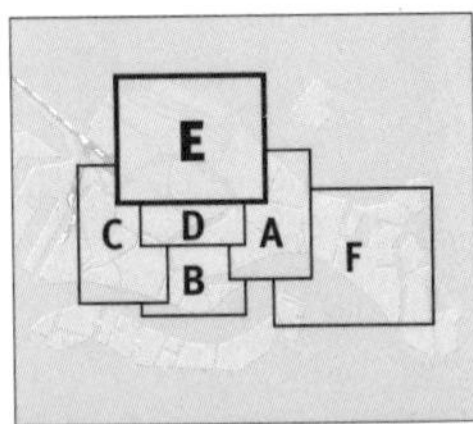

DA'A MARISA

ALLA VEDOVA

RESTAURANTS

Gam Gam (**E** B2)
→ *Cannaregio 1122, Fondamenta di Cannaregio*
Tel. 041 275 92 56
Sun-Thu 10am–10pm (and Sat night in winter, depending on the Sabbath)
To make a change from polenta and sardines, this restaurant offers Israeli specialties that have gained popularity with the locals. Falafel, hummus, soups, moussaka and schnitzels. Entrées €7.50–22.

Da'a Marisa (**E** A2)
→ *Cannaregio 652, Fondamenta di San Giobbe*
Tel. 041 72 02 11
Tue, Thu-Sat noon–2.30pm, 7.30–11pm; Wed, Sun-Mon noon–2.30pm
No need to ask for the menu – there isn't one. Service is fast and you have to choose quickly between the two or three dishes of the day prepared according to the chef's inspiration and what the local market has to offer. A genuine Italian canteen. Prix fixe (lunch) €15; entrées €10–20.

Alla Vedova (**E** E4)
→ *Cannaregio 3912, Ramo Ca' d'Oro; Tel. 041 528 53 24; Mon-Wed, Fri-Sat 11.30am–2.30pm, 6.30–10.30pm; Sun 6.30–10.30pm (closed Aug)*
Reminiscent of a tavern, this is one of the most famous osterie in the district, serving up excellent traditional cuisine to eat at the counter; large choice of *cicchetti* and *polpette*. Entrées €11–14.

Da Rioba (**E** D2)
→ *Cannaregio 2552, Fondamenta della Misericordia*
Tel 041 524 43 79
Tue-Sun 12.30–2.30pm, 7.30–10.30pm (closed Jan and Aug)
This small, traditional restaurant gives pride of place to fish and seafood, which it turns into simple but flavorsome dishes with an elaborate twist that sets them apart. Terrace along the canal in summer. Friendly service. Entrées €9–24.

Antica Adelaide (**E** E3)
→ *Cannaregio 3728, Calle Priuli; Tel. 041 523 26 29*
Daily 10am–3.30pm, 6–11pm
The kitchen in this 18th-c palace is visible from the street, revealing a chef who concocts exquisite, inventive dishes: salmon baked in sesame pastry, pear ravioli with sage and

PARLAMENTO

PARADISO PERDUTO

NICOLAO ATELIER

poppy seeds. Entrées €11–30.

Vini da Gigio (**E** E3)
→ *Cannaregio 3628/A, Fondamenta di San Felice Tel. 041 528 51 40; Wed-Sun 12.30–2.30pm, 7–10.30pm*
A simple, friendly trattoria with a fabulous wine list (over 500 on the menu) and excellent seasonal cuisine: grilled *anguilla*, *seppia alla veneziana*, or deep-fried soft-shell crabs (*moeche*). Entrées €13–20.

PATISSERIE, BARS, MOVIE THEATER

Dal Mas (**E** A3)
→ *Cannaregio 150/A, Rio Terrà, Lista di Spagna Tel 041 71 51 01; Daily 7am (7.30am Sun)–8pm*
Near the Ponte dei Scalzi and the train station, it is one of the city's oldest patisseries (1853). Coffee at the counter and take-out delicacies.

Cantina Vecia Carbonera (**E** D3)
→ *Cannaregio 2329, Campo della Maddalena Tel. 041 71 03 76; Tue-Sun 9am–10pm (11am–3pm, –11pm in winter)*
This former coal cellar has been furnished informally with wooden tables and barrels. There is a good selection of wines and delicious *cicchetti*.

Frulalà (**E** D3)
→ *Cannaregio 2235/B, Strada Nova; Sun-Fri 9am–midnight (8pm Fri, 4pm Fri in winter); Sat 6pm–2am*
This eye-catching kiosk on a pedestrian street offers fresh fruit juices, yoghurts and smoothies.

Bar al Parlamento (**E** A2)
→ *Cannaregio 511, Fondamenta Savorgnan Tel. 041 244 02 14; Daily 7.30am–2am (8.30am Sun)*
The rather boisterous rallying point for the local university students. Varied music and concerts every ten days or so.

Paradiso Perduto (**E** D2)
→ *Cannaregio 2540, Fondamenta della Misericordia Tel. 041 72 05 81 Thu 6pm–midnight; Fri-Sun noon–1am (midnight Sun)*
Perduto? Not for the night owls who revel in this spacious bar-restaurant with long tables and a pretty waterside terrace. Lively atmosphere, especially at the concerts on the weekend.

Giorgione Movie d'Essai (**E** E4)
→ *Cannaregio 4612/A, Rio Terrà dei Franceschi Tel. 041 522 62 98; around 5pm, 7.30pm and 9.30pm*
The last independent movie theater in Venice, with two screens for art-house cinema.

SHOPPING

Nicolao Atelier (**E** D2)
→ *Cannaregio 2590, Fondamenta della Misericordia Tel. 041 520 97 49; Mon-Fri 9.30am–1pm, 2.30–6pm*
The costume designer for the movies *Farinelli* and *The Merchant of Venice* sells and rents costumes and accessories for the Carnival.

El Papussa Calegher (**E** D2)
→ *Cannaregio 2612, Fondamenta della Misericordia Tel. 041 524 22 48; Mon-Fri 10am–1pm, 3.30–7.30pm; Sat 10am–1pm*
The long strips of leather hanging from the ceiling provide the raw material for *papusse* (traditional Venetian pants), as well as belts, bags and sandals.

The Studio in Venice (**E** B2)
→ *Cannaregio 1152; Calle del Ghetto Vecchio; Tel. 041 520 89 97; Sun-Fri 9.30am–7.30pm (4.30pm in winter)*
The colorful, naive paintings by Michal Meron depict scenes from the life of Venice's Jewish community, as well as religious holidays and episodes from the Torah.

Stamperia del Ghetto (**E** B2)
→ *Cannaregio 1185/A, Calle del Ghetto Vecchio Tel. 041 275 02 00 Sun-Fri 10am–5pm*
Souvenirs from the Jewish Ghetto: views of Venice by the painter Emanuele Luzzati, carved wood, bookmarks with Hebrew characters, etc.

Mori & Bozzi (**E** D3)
→ *Cannaregio 2367, Rio Terrà della Maddalena Tel. 041 71 52 61 Mon-Sat 9.30am–7.30pm, Sun 11am–7pm (closed Sun July-Aug)*
A fashionable, sophisticated boutique selling original Italian clothes, shoes and accessories.

Torrefazione Cannaregio (**E** C3)
→ *Cannaregio 1337, Rio Terrà San Leonardo Tel. 041 71 63 71 Mon-Sat 7am–7.30pm; Sun 9.30am–1pm, 2–6.30pm*
One of the two roasters left in Venice, it has been importing coffee since 1930. Take out or drink on the premises.

I SAN GEREMIA

CHIESA DEGLI SCALZI

D E F

1

2

CANALE DELLE NAVI

ORTO

R. I° PIAVE

R. II° PIAVE

SCUOLA DEI MERCANTI

★ CHIESA DELLA MADONNA DELL'ORTO

Campo della Madonna dell'Orto

FOND. DELLA MADONNA DELL'ORTO

CAMPO DEI MORI

★ PALAZZO MASTELLI

FOND. GASPARO CONTARINI

C. ARRIGONI

CALLE BRASO

FOND. DEI MORI

C. LONGO

CALLE DEL CALDERER

C. GROPPI

RIO DELLA SENSA

C. D. FORNER

RAMO DEI MUTI

RIO DEI MUTI

CORTE VECCHIA

SACCA DELLA MISERICORDIA

FONDAMENTA DELLA MISERICORDIA

RIO DELLA MISERICORDIA

C. D. PIGNATE

C. D. ZOCCOLO

CALLE TREVISAN

FOND. DELL'ABBAZIA

ABBAZIA VECCHIA DELLA MISERICORDIA

S. MARIA VALVERDE

SOTTOP. DELL'ABBAZIA

C. LARGA LEZZE

FOND. MORO

Campo S. Marziale

CALLE ZANCANI

FOND. DEL TRAPOLIN

Campo della Maddalena

Campo di Sta. Fosca

S. FOSCA

FOND. DELL'ABBAZIA

CANALE DELLA MISERICORDIA

C. BOLDU

CALLE LUNGA

S. CATERINA

C. D. MASENA

FOND. S. CATERINA

RIO SANTA CATERINA

FONDAMENTE NOVE

CALLE MARCO FOSCARINI

C. D. CADENE

C. D. LEGNAMI

S. D. BOTTERI

C. D. CROCIFERI

I GESUITI

A MARIA SERVI

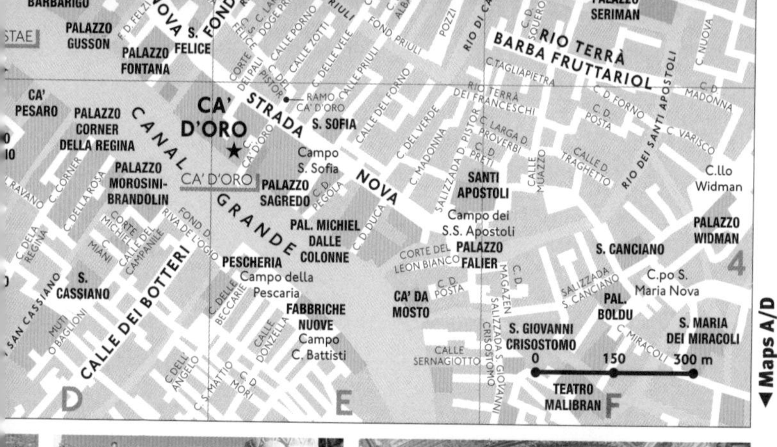

CAMPO DEI MORI

I GESUITI

Daily 10am (noon
n
ant red-brick
; a blend of styles:
nce portal,
sque alcoves, little
ches. Inside is a
seum to Tintoretto,
the chapel, who
some of his most
works here (*The*
nent, 1562).
dei
i (**E** A2)
he originality and
of this three-
idge (1688), it
r copied, as it
he traffic and
rom the canal
e Lagoon.

★ **Museo Ebraico e Sinagoghe** (**E** C2)
→ *Cannaregio 2902/B, Campo del Ghetto Nuovo Tel. 041 71 53 59; Sun-Fri 10am–7pm (5.30pm Oct-May)*
When a Senate decree assigned the Jews residing in Venice to a specific residential zone, in 1516, they created the first ghetto of the Western world. As the population grew in this restricted space, the city's tallest buildings were erected. The museum retains cult objects, and its visit includes the five synagogues, the most impressive of which is the Scuola Levantina (1538).

★ **Chiesa di Sant'Alvise** (**E** C1)
→ *Cannaregio 3282, Campo di Sant'Alvise; Mon-Sat 10am–5pm (see Chorus in Practical Venice)*
Venice's most remote church, medieval in style (1388). The diminutive entrance hides a baroque interior with a trompe-l'œil ceiling and frescos by G. B. Tiepolo (1740).

★ **Campo dei Mori** (**E** D2)
Built into the walls of the square are three 13th-c. statues representing the Mastelli brothers, who came from Morea in the Peloponnese, in the 12th century. The most famous, known as *Sior Antonio Rioba*, depicted with an iron nose, was the spokesman for the Venetians in criticizing the Republic.

★ **I Gesuiti** (**E** F3)
→ *Cannaregio, Campo dei Gesuiti; Tel. 041 528 65 79 Daily 10am–noon, 3.30–5pm*
In 1715 Rossi was commissioned to rebuild this Jesuit church to reflect the glory of the order at a time when it was not very popular. The result was a lavish baroque façade and impressive interior: stucco, multicolored marble on the pulpit and a huge canopy. Inside is Titian's *Martyrdom of St Lawrence*.

MUSEO STORICO NAVALE

GIARDINI PUBBLICI E BIENNALE

PONTE DI QUINTAVALLE

★ **Scuola di San Giorgio degli Schiavoni** (**F** B2)
→ *Castello 3259/A, Calle dei Furlani; Tel. 041 522 88 28*
Mon 2.45–6pm; Tue-Sat 9.15am–1pm, 2.45–6pm; Sun 9.15am–1pm
In 1502 the influential Dalmatian order commissioned Carpaccio to do a series of paintings depicting the lives of its patron saints. One of them is the famous *St George and the Dragon* (1507).

★ **Chiesa di San Zaccaria** (**F** A2)
→ *Castello 4693, Campo San Zaccaria; Tel 041 522 12 57*
Mon-Sat 10am–noon, 4–6pm; Sun 4–6pm
The incredible richness of this Renaissance sanctuary is thanks to the generosity of the wealthy families of the nuns from the nearby convent. The Golden Chapel houses rare treasures of sculpted wood and the crypt where the bodies of eight doges are laid to rest. Altarpiece by Bellini, paintings by Vivarini and Giovanni d'Alemagna.

★ **Chiesa di San Francesco della Vigna** (**F** B1)
→ *Castello 2786, Campo San Francesco della Vigna*
Tel. 041 520 61 02
Daily 8am–12.30pm, 3–7pm
The grapevine (*vigna*) that grew on the campo has now disappeared. The façade of this church (16th c.), by Palladio, is a model of classicism, displaying an architectural harmony of alternating triangles and rectangles. Look out for Veronese's altarpiece (1551).

★ **Torri dell'Arsenale** (**F** C2)
Two red-brick turrets mark the (sea) entrance to the Arsenal, an old shipyard encased in tall ramparts. Next to it, on dry ground, a magnificent Renaissance gateway (1460) is framed by two white marble lions, brought back from Morea in 1687. The first ind shipyard in the worl (13th c.) used to be a forbidden zone. Now a military base, it op some of its 113 acres public during the Bi

★ **Riva degli Schiavoni** (**F** A2)
This stylish waterfro promenade is lined with prestigious hot including the famou Danieli, once the ro hideout of Alfred de Musset and George

★ **Museo Storico Navale** (**F** C3)
→ *Castello 2148, Riva Biagio; Tel. 041 244 1*
Mon-Thu 8.45am–1.3

CHIESA DI SAN ZACCARIA

RIVA DEGLI SCHIAVONI

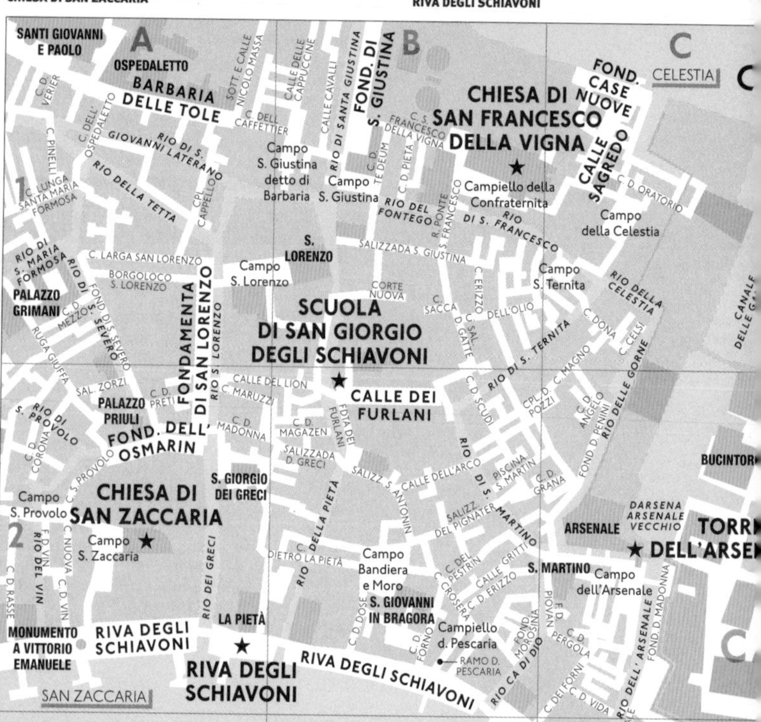

Venetians claim that their city is shaped like a fish, with Cannaregio as its backbone and Castello as the tail. From the Calle Lunga Santa Maria Formosa (to the west), filled with *osterias* and small shops, to the mercantile Via Garibaldi (to the east), via the Arsenal and its empty building sites, Castello, often overlooked by visitors, has retained its working-class soul. To the southeast, bordering the Lagoon, the Giardini Pubblici comes to life during the Biennale of contemporary art. On the opposite shore is the island of San Giorgio Maggiore and its imposing basilica.

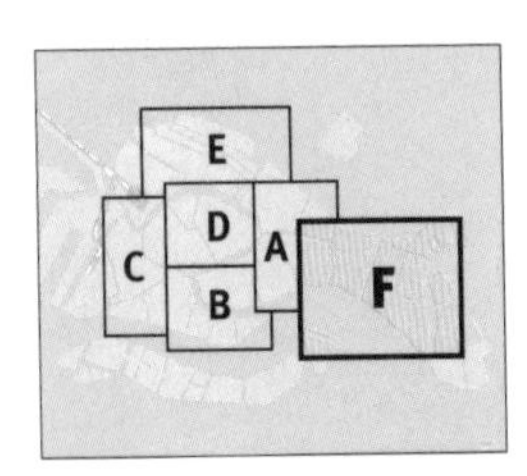

DA REMIGIO

AL COVO

RESTAURANTS

Trattoria alla Rivetta (**F** A2)
→ *Castello 4625, Ponte San Provolo; Tel. 041 528 73 02 Tue-Sun 10am–11pm*
The gondoliers' cafeteria is well known for its *cicchetti*. Stand at the diminutive counter for slices of eggplant and mozzarella, *sarde in saor* and grilled vegetables. There's also a large dining room where you can sample the house special: *bigoli in salsa* (anchovy pasta). Entrées €8–20.

Le Spighe (**F** D3)
→ *Castello 1341, Via Garibaldi; Tel. 041 523 81 73 Mon-Sat 10am–2.30pm, 5.30–7.30pm*
This restaurant-grocery store offers innovative vegetarian food made with organic ingredients. The formula is simple: pick dishes from the menu and then pay for them according to their weight – before eating them on the spot or taking them away. Entrées €10–15.

Da Remigio (**F** B2)
→ *Castello 3416, Salizzada dei Greci; Tel. 041 523 00 89 Mon 12.30–2.30pm; Wed-Sun 12.30–2pm, 7.30–10pm*
There's nothing special about the decor in this trattoria but the food more than makes up for it. Excellent seafood: *gnocchi alla pescatora*, grilled squid and scampi, etc. Entrées €10–25.

Corte Sconta (**F** B2)
→ *Castello 3886, Calle del Pestrin Tel. 041 522 70 24; Tue-Sat 12.30–2pm, 7–9.30pm; closed in Jan and Aug*
Fans of the character Corto Maltese will recognize the 'secret courtyard' featured in the comic-strip series. Others will fall for the elegant seafood cuisine, lauded by Venetians: sautéed clams with ginger; risotto with scampi. Fine wine list, too. Entrées €18–28.

Al Covo (**F** B2)
→ *Castello 3968, Campiello della Pescaria Tel. 041 522 38 12; Fri-Tue 12.45–2pm, 7.30–10pm*
Both simple and refined, this is one of the favorite hangouts of celebrities, and perfect for a romantic occasion. Ingredients are fresh, locally sourced and dishes are beautifully presented. They include fried soft-shell crabs (*moeche*), fish tartares, roast lamb with lentils. Entrées €20–33.

A FORST

BRAGORÀ

MURANERO

CAFÉS, BARS, ICE-CREAM PARLOR

Mela Verde (F A2)
→ *Castello 4977, ondamenta dell'Osmarin el. 349 195 79 24)aily 11am–10pm 7pm Oct-Nov)*
his ice-cream parlor as built its reputation n sorbets, made in ouse with seasonal ruit: grapefruit, kiwi, etc.

a Mascareta (**F** A1)
→ *Castello 5183, Calle unga Santa Maria Formosa el. 041 523 07 44 aily 7pm–2am*
his wine bar holds its wn against more famous ocal rivals. It has become hotspot for wine lovers nd stays buzzing until ne early hours. Snacks n the side: cooked neats, cheese and *cchetti*.

1 Paradiso (**F** E4)
→ *Castello 1260, iardini Pubblici; Tel. 41 241 39 72; Daily 8am–om; closed Dec to mid-Feb*
n elegant café within ne gardens of the Venice iennale. You can take our place at the counter, the large dining room, on any of the three rraces, one of which is 1 the roof, overlooking e Lagoon.

Birreria Forst (**F** A2)
→ *Castello 4540, Calle delle Rasse Tel. 041 523 05 57 Daily 9am–11pm*
Away from the hustle and bustle of the tourists but still close to St Mark's, this bar is the perfect place for a snack and aperitif with the gondoliers.

La Serra dei Giardini (**F** D3)
→ *Castello 1254 Viale Garibaldi Tel. 041 296 03 60; Tue-Sun 9am (11am Nov-Dec, Feb-March)–8pm*
A tearoom inside a greenhouse, with tables set amongst the plants, and more outside on the grass. Savory pies and sandwiches, organic wine by the glass, teas and fresh juices.

Ai Do Pozzi (**F** B2)
→ *Castello 2613, Campiello do Pozzi Tel. 041 520 71 41 Daily 9am–1am*
An authentic neighborhood bar run by two young women (hence the bar's nickname of '*Dae Fie*': the girls' place). Locals come here to read newspapers over a coffee or to play chess. Pretty terrace on a quiet square; concerts.

SHOPPING

Libreria Acqua Alta (**F** A1)
→ *Castello 5176/B, Calle Lunga Santa Maria Formosa Daily 9am–8pm*
A treasure trove presided over by a cigar-smoking bookseller whose books are piled up precariously in every nook and cranny – even inside a gondola! The door at the back opens onto a canal, which makes it a precarious place to be at times of *acqua alta*!

Bragorà (**F** B2)
→ *Castello 3496, Salizzada Sant'Antonin Tel. 041 319 08 64 Mon-Sat 9.30am–7.30pm; Sun 10.30am–6.30pm*
A cross between a store and an art gallery, Bragorà exhibits the work of young local artists who transform objects to give them a new use: bicycle tubes become belts, and sails are turned into bags.

Vino e Vini (**F** B2)
→ *Castello 3566, Salizzada del Pignater Tel. 041 521 01 84 Mon-Sat 9.30am–1pm, 5–8pm (8.30pm in summer)*
Grapevines actually grow outside this enoteca, which offers an exhaustive selection of Venetian wines, some 85 types of *grappa* and some fine table wines served straight from the pump.

Muranero (**F** B2)
→ *Castello 3545, Salizzada del Pignater; Tel. 338 450 30 99; Daily 11am–8pm*
Trained at the Murano glass school, Niang Moulaye has moved on to create his own designs of African-inspired glass jewelry, including bracelets, necklaces and rings.

Il Mercante Veneziano (**F** C3)
→ *Castello 2139, Riva San Biágio; Tel. 041 520 59 90 Daily 11am–2pm, 3.30–11pm (8pm in winter)*
Roberto Bisutti produces stylish leather articles (diaries, notebooks), as well as high-class stationery and reproductions of classic prints.

Barbieri (**F** A2)
→ *Castello 3403, Calle della Madonna Tel. 041 522 81 77 Mon-Sat 10am–12.30pm, 3.30–7.30pm*
A reputed but accessibly priced Venetian brand of fashion accessories for men and women; scarves, shawls, ties and blouses made from linen, silk, wool and cashmere.

DI SAN GIORGIO DEGLI SCHIAVONI

CHIESA DI SAN FRANCESCO DELLA VIGNA

TORRI DELL'ARSENALE

D
E
F
1
2

E DELLE NAVI
BACINI

CAMPO SPORTIVO
BACINI DI CARENAGGIO
CANALE DI PORTA NUOVA
DARSENA GRANDE
RIO DELLE VERGINI
CANALE DI SAN PIETRO
RIO SAN DANIELE
C. LARGA S. PIETRO
C. D. FIGHER
C. D. TERCO
SALIZZADA STRETTA
CANALE DI SAN PIETRO
CAMPO SAN PIETRO
CHIESA ★ DI SAN PIETRO DI CASTELLO
LLO
CORDERIE
FOND. RIELLO FORNER
CALLE MARAFANI
C. SALOMON
C. D. BIANCO
FOND. QUINTAVALLE
ISOLA DI SAN PIETRO
FOND. CASTELOLNOLO
RIO DELLA TANA
FOND. DELLA TANA
C. DEL PRETI
C. COLTERRA
C. S. FRANCESCO
SAN FRANCESCO DI PAOLA
C. S. ANNA
CALLE QUINTAVALLE ★
PONTE DI QUINTAVALLE
FOND. SAN GIOACCHINO
FOND. SANT'ANNA
EX CHIESA
RIO DI QUINTAVALLE

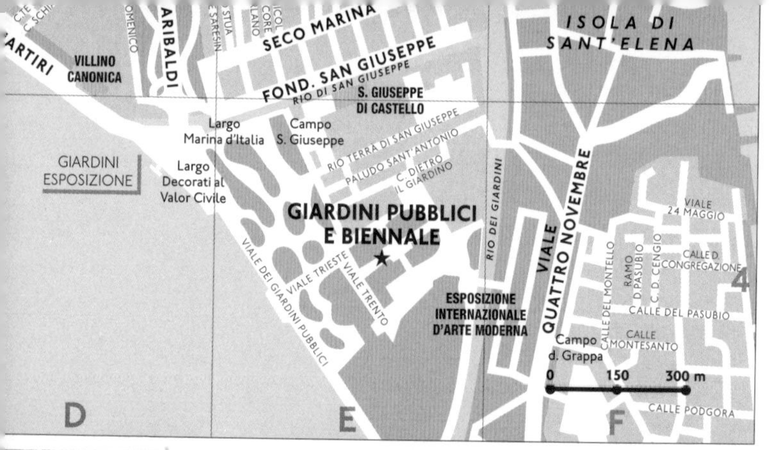

SAN PIETRO DI CASTELLO

BASILICA DI SAN GIORGIO MAGGIORE

m–5pm (5.30pm in ; Sun 10am–5pm in summer)
perty of the Italian nice's Naval holds an amazing f weapons and dels, as well as ntation relating ian expeditions t naval battles.

ini Pubblici ale (**F** E4)
ei Giardini Pubblici
21 87 11
e.org
astern tip of the one of Venice's ic gardens, n 1811 under 's initiative. From June to November it welcomes the Biennale of contemporary art (every odd year since 1895), and the Biennale of architecture (every even year). The 29 pavilions built by famous architects (Carlo Scarpa for Venezuela, Alvar Aalto for Finland...) can be visited during those events only.

★ Ponte di Quintavalle (**F** E3)
Inaugurated in 2009, this fine wooden bridge took the place of one that was no longer safe. A link to the island of San Pietro, it symbolizes the authorities' efforts to regenerate the Castello district.

★ Chiesa di San Pietro di Castello (**F** F2)
→ Castello 72, Campo San Pietro; Mon-Sat 10–5pm (see Chorus in Practical Venice)
Built on San Pietro island, this isolated sanctuary, dating back to the 7th century, was Venice's cathedral from 1451 to 1807, at which date it was supplanted by San Marco. Behind an imposing façade inspired by Palladio (1596) is a marble altar and, in the Lando chapel, an altarpiece with mosaic by Zuccato, after a drawing by Tintoretto.

★ Basilica di San Giorgio Maggiore (**F** A4)
→ Isola di San Giorgio Maggiore; Tel 041 522 78 27 Daily 9.30am–7pm (5pm in winter)
On this small island is one of Palladio's last masterpieces, started in 1566. Its façade draws inspiration from classical temples. Inside, the chorus is adorned with famous paintings by Tintoretto (*Fall of Manna* on the left and *The Last Supper* on the right) and, in the Conclave, Carpaccio's altarpiece (1516). Panoramic views over the Lagoon and San Marco from the bell tower.

AIRPORT LINKS

Aeroporto Marco Polo
By bus
→ *Every 20–30 mins to Piazzale Roma* (**C** B2)*; journey 20 mins; single €6 or €4 with tourist ticket*
By boat (waterbus)
→ *alilaguna.it*
Departs every 30–60 mins toward San Marco; journey 1hr 15 mins; €27 return (€25 if booked online)
By taxi
→ *€40; journey 20 mins to Piazzale Roma*
By water-taxi
→ *€110; journey 30 mins*
Aeroporto di Treviso
By bus
→ *Departs every 25 mins; 1hr 10 mins; €7*

VAPORETTO APPROACHING THE RIALTO BRIDGE

TAXI-BOAT IN FRONT OF SANTA LUCIA STATION

rooms and great service. €60–160.

Pausania (**B** A2)
→ *Dorsoduro 2824, Fondamenta Gherardini Tel. 041 522 20 83 hotelpausania.it*
A stunning 14th-century Venetian palace with Gothic windows, wooden ceilings, a beautiful well in the garden and all modern comforts. The rooms overlooking the patio are quieter than those on the small canal. €65–240.

€80–150

Casa Kirsch (**A** C5)
→ *Castello 4266, Calle dei Albanesi; Tel. 041 528 61 27 casakirsch.com*
A modern, designer B&B with exposed beams, king-sized beds, flat plasma screens and internet access in each of the three elegant bedrooms. Buffet breakfast is served at the sister hotel Casa Verardo, 50 yards away. €80–280.

A le Boteghe (**B** C1)
→ *San Marco 3438, Calle delle Botteghe; Tel. 349 197 4833; aleboteghe.it*
A B&B on the second floor of a Venetian palace, comprising two twin rooms and one triple, all with modern comforts. Copious breakfast, and a lovely hostess, Clara. €90–115.

Foresteria Valdese (**A** C3)
→ *Castello 5170, Fondamente Cavagnis; Tel. 041 528 67 97 foresteriavenezia.it*
A 16th-century palace for those on a budget. Choice of twin rooms, dormitory rooms or two apartments. Rambling but splendid. €32–35 (dorm); €100–140 (double).

La Fenice (**B** E2)
→ *San Marco 1936, Campiello Fenice Tel. 041 523 23 33 fenicehotels.com*
This traditional hotel doesn't lack charm but its main asset is an excellent location, on a small square near the opera house. Some preference for the rooms of the hotel's old wing. €90–320.

San Moisè (**B** F2)
→ *San Marco 2058, Piscina San Moisè; Tel. 041 520 37 55 sanmoise.it*
This elegant 18th-century former convent in a quiet narrow street has retained its character with high ceilings, original stuccos and Murano lamps. Some of the 16 sunny rooms overlook the canal that borders the house. €90–700.

Galleria (**B** C3)
→ *Dorsoduro 878/A, Rio Terrà A. Foscarini; Tel. 041 523 24 89; hotelgalleria.it*
In a most beautiful, Venetian-style 17th-century palace close to

TRAINS AND BUSES

Rail links
Santa Lucia Station (**C** B1)
Not to be confused with the **Venezia-Mestre** station built on the mainland, **Santa Lucia** is built on the Lagoon.
→ *Tel. 041 78 56 70/89 20 21*
London–Venice
By Orient Express train
→ *Tel. 0845 077 2222 orient-express.com*
By Eurostar to Paris
→ *Tel. 08432 186 186 eurostar.com*
Paris–Venice
Daily, overnight train; 12 hours.
→ *SNCF (French railways); voyages-sncf.com*
Venice–Italy
Regular trains to Milan, Turin, Bologna, Florence and Rome.
→ *trenitalia.com*

VENICE BY ROAD

By car
Cars must be left at the entrance to the city. Parking is expensive (around €21/ 24 hours)
→ *veniceparking.it*
Autorimessa Tronchetto
→ *Isola del Tronchetto Tel. 041 520 75 55; 24/7*
Autorimessa Comunale
→ *Piazzale Roma, 496 Tel. 041 272 72 11; 24/7*
Parcheggio Sant'Andrea
→ *Piazzale Roma Tel. 041 272 73 04; 24/7*
By bus
Lines (ACTV) operate between Piazzale Roma and Mestre.
By taxi
→ *Tel. 041 595 20 80*
For traveling outside of the Lagoon area only.

AIRPORTS

Aeroporto Marco Polo
→ *Tel. 041 260 92 60*
veniceairport.it
In Tessera, 7½ miles north of the city. Direct flights to various major Italian and European cities.
Lost luggage
→ *Tel. 041 260 92 22*
Daily 9am–7pm
Aeroporto di Treviso
→ *Tel. 042 231 51 11*
trevisoairport.it
In Treviso, 25 miles to the northwest of Venice. The airport of the low-cost airlines (inc. Ryanair; German Wings)

ACCESS TO AIRPORTS

- *Prices given (low season-high season) are for a double room en suite, breakfast included. A tourist tax will be added to the price (between €0.5 and €5 per person per day)*
- *Reserve at least three months in advance for visits in July-Aug and during Carnival (Feb).*

Associazione Veneziana Albergatori (AVA)
→ *Tel. 041 522 22 64*
avanews.it
Can assist in finding accommodation; charges a €2 fee per booking.
VeneziaSi
→ *Tel. 041 522 22 64*
veneziasi.it
Has 450 hotels to search and book online.
Renting an apartment
Live like a Venetian for a few days in a studio or a luxurious palace. From €90 per day, depending on the season.
→ *venice-rentals.com*
→ *veniceapartment.com*
→ *airbnb.com*

UNDER €80

Locanda Montin (C D5)
→ *Dorsoduro 1147, Fondamenta di Borgo Tel. 041 522 71 51 locandamontin.com*
Opposite the tranquil Romite canal, this inn has a private garden and a good restaurant set under an arbor. The rooms are plain but peace and quiet are guaranteed. €50–160.
B&B Sandra (E D3)
→ *Cannaregio 2452, Corte Trapolin; Tel. 041 72 09 57 bbalessandra.com*
Alessandra ('Sandra'), and Leonardo rent two rooms and a suite of their elegant 17th-century house. Wonderful hosts, they'll introduce you to Venetian food and initiate you to the city's secrets while you sip a glass of Prosecco on the *altana* (the traditional Venetian wooden roof terrace) with views over Venice. €75–150.
Barababao (A A3)
→ *Cannaregio 5835, Calle Corte del Milion; Tel. 349 877 80 19; barababao.it*
A small, friendly B&B whose owners – a father and his two sons– also run the (quiet) bar below. Peaceful, and yet only two steps away from the Rialto. Excellent value for money. €50–150.
Pensione Guerrato (D E3)
→ *San Polo 240/A, Calle Drio la Scimia Tel. 041 528 59 27 pensioneguerrato.it*
A pleasant hotel behind the Rialto market. Nineteen light, airy rooms €100–145; €75–100 (shared bathroom).
Ai do Mori (A B5)
→ *San Marco 658, Calle Larga San Marco; Tel. 041 520 48 17 hotelaidomori.com*
Fourteen small but cozy rooms close to St Marks Square, all with TV and a conditioning. Some have a view of the Campanile. The nicest (no. 11) has a private terrace. €50–15 (without breakfast).
Ca' Turelli (C D5)
→ *Dorsoduro 1162, Fondamenta di Borgo; Tel. 348 303 46 88; caturelli.it*
A large B&B close to the Ponte dell'Accademia. Th three modern bedrooms are spacious and soberly decorated. Hearty buffet breakfast in the large communal room. €70–13
Istituto Ciliota (B C2)
→ *San Marco 2976, Calle delle Muneghe; Tel. 041 520 48 88; ciliota.it*
A peaceful haven in a former convent tucked away in a pretty courtyard Rather nondescript deco but 34 (51 in summer) spacious, air-conditioned

Best of the best

What you have to experience in Venice

Breakfast in a café
Venetians stick to the traditional Italian ways of doing things, and grabbing a bite of breakfast on the way to work is one of them. A strong black coffee at the counter with a bun (such as the popular s-shaped *bussola*, which evokes the contours of the Grand Canal) is the usual way to get the day going here.
→ *At the Rizzardini* (**D** D3) or *Rosa Salva* (**A** C3)

Go paddling at high tide (acqua alta)
Much of Venice is flooded when the water rises in winter, enthralling visitors but frustating the locals, who are forced to barricade the entrance to their houses (shopkeepers are warned by text message). Sirens announce the rising of the waters, with different signals conveying the gravity of the situation (the longer the series of whistles, the greater the danger).
→ *Think about rubber boots if you're visiting in winter*

Treat yourself to a carnival mask
Venice is essentially a small town where you can expect to meet the same people repeatedly. Carnival, which in former times could last for up to six months, allowed people to merge invisibly into the background, the nobility to move about unrecognized and libertines to indulge their passions. The masks they wore guaranteed anonymity. Nowadays Carnival only lasts a few weeks but the enthusiasm has not abated. Every mask tells a story: that of the 'doctor', with its long pointed nose, was stuffed with medicinal plants to protect against the germs of his patients.
→ *Authentic masks are made from papier mâché, such as those from Ca' Macana* (**C** D5)

Drink a Spritz or a Bellini
Originally introduced by the Hapsburgs, Spritz has become easily the most popular local aperitif at 6pm in bars all over the city. The recipe for this cocktail consists of a third sparkling water (Seltz for the purists), a third dry white wine (Prosecco) and a third bitter alcohol such as Aperol or Campari, with a slice of lemon and a small olive to finish off. Alternative cocktails include the Bellini (the real thing should be champagne and fresh peach juice), preferably drunk at Harry's Bar (**A** A6).

ACQUA ALTA

CICCHETTI

MIXING A SPRITZ

GONDOLA

→ *In winter, try the bars next to the Rialto market* (**D** F4) *and, in summer, the ones at Campo Santa Margherita* (**C** C4)

Shop at the Rialto market
Bitter red chicory (*radicchio*), pale green cabbage (*romanesco*), young purple artichokes (*castraure*): the vegetables at the Rialto (**D** E2) are perfect photo opportunities. The covered fish market is another delight, with the night's catch from the Lagoon on display.
→ *9am or earlier is best; the stalls pack up around 11am*

Use public transportation
Getting around needn't be expensive. The *traghetti* – large, hefty gondolas – will take you from one *sestiere* to another for the price of an espresso. The motor boats (*vaporetti*), which follow the curves of the Grand Canal to all parts of the city, cost a little more.
→ *Be sure to take change onboard; some traghetti routes run mornings only*

Take a ride on a gondola
Exploring the canals on a gondola is like passing through the arteries of the city deep into its hidden recesses; rocked by the waves and soothed by the splashing of the oars, it's a world away from the crowded streets. Touristy maybe, but unique, and a great way to see the city from the water.
→ *Fixed prices (depending on the option chosen)*

Eat like the Venetians
In their lunch break around noon, Venetians eat *tramezzini* (crustless sandwiches) or *cicchetti* (snacks similar to tapas): fast food and good value. Eat more subtantially in the evenings at a trattoria. Try some local specialities such as black spaghetti with squid ink, liver *alla veneziana* or sardines *in saor* (marinated in vinegar).

Laze about at the Lido
Venice's own seaside: a thin strip of land reached by *vaporetto* and extending for 7 miles between the Lagoon and the Adriatic. The resort's clear waters make it very popular in the summer, not surprisingly. *Good sunbathing at Alberoni beach or on the island of Pellestrina (bus no. 11)*

Go to the opera at La Fenice (**B** E2)
The destruction of La Fenice by fire in 1996 shocked not only Venetians but the whole world, and its new replacement is an exact copy of the original. This heroic achievement was finally completed in 2004, bringing one of Italy's most famous opera houses back to life.
→ *Reserve several weeks in advance*

ARNIVAL

FLOATING MARKET, CAMPO SAN BARBARA

OOLIER

GHETTO ON THE GRAND CANAL

GONDOLA

tury *palazzo*, tucked
› a quiet street near
Accademia. Art Deco
niture, Turkish baths,
and restaurant, roof
ace. €115–630.

'ER €150

i Alboretti (**B** B3)
Dorsoduro 884,
Terrà Antonio Foscarini
041 523 00 58
ialboretti.com
y a few minutes from
Accademia, 22 bright
d pretty but fairly small
ms behind a handsome
ck façade; also has two
tes. Good restaurant
d a flowered courtyard.
60–460.
nsione La
lcina (**B** B4)
Dorsoduro 780,
ndamenta Zattere ai
suati; Tel. 041 520 64 66
alcina.com
so called Ruskin's
use, as John Ruskin
stayed here in 1876.
Parquet flooring, simple, refined decor in each of the 27 rooms, some with views of the Giudecca. In season, breakfast is served on the terrace overlooking the Canal and Giudecca island. €150–350.

Pensione Accademia – Villa Maravege (**B** B2)
→ *Dorsoduro 1058, Fondamenta Bollani*
Tel. 041 521 01 88
pensioneaccademia.it
A gem of a guesthouse in a splendid 17th-century villa by a small canal near the Accademia bridge. Twenty-seven airy rooms, and a gorgeous garden with deckchairs; very peaceful. €155–400.

Metropole (**F** B2)
→ *Castello 4149, Riva degli Schiavoni; Tel. 041 520 5044*
hotelmetropole.com
Absolute luxury and perfect attention to detail in this antique-laden palace, where each room is unique in style and decoration. Has a garden and breathtaking views over the Lagoon. Michelin-starred restaurant. €175–500.

LUXURY HOTELS

Danieli (**F** B2)
→ *Castello 4196, Riva degli Schiavoni*
Tel. 041 522 64 80
danieli.hotelvenice.com
Marble, sumptuous crystal chandeliers and arcaded staircases – this hotel is considered to be something of a monument. €485–1600.

The Gritti Palace (**B** E2)
→ *San Marco 2467, Campo Santa Maria del Giglio*
Tel. 041 79 46 11
thegrittipalace.com
A 16th-century palace favored by Ruskin and Hemingway. €425–1800.

BY BOAT

By vaporetto
'Vaporetto' generally refers to any type of water transport: technically speaking, a *vaporetto* is a wide, slow-moving boat, a *motoscafo* is narrower and lower, and a *motonave* is a type of ferry. They operate 24/7 (four night-time lines) throughout the city and the northern islands: Murano, Burano, etc.

Information (ACTV)
(C B2)
→ *Piazzale Roma*
Tel. 041 2424; actv.it

Ticket sales
Onboard, at major stops, tourist offices and tobacconists.
→ *€7/1 hr*
→ *Line 1: €4/trip*
→ *Tourist ticket (results in savings after two journeys): €18/12hrs; €20/24hrs; €30/48hrs; add €4 to include travel to/ from the airport*

Rolling Venice Card
→ *€20/72 hrs*
A travel card for 14–29 year olds.

Season tickets
From the ACTV, Piazzale Roma.
→ *€40 for the card; offers reduced fares (€1.30 for a single journey; €30 for a monthly travel pass)*

By traghetto
Shared gondolas act as bridges between the shores of the Grand Canal.
→ *Crossing €2 (€0.70 with a season ticket)*

By water-taxi
→ *Tel. 041 522 23 03*
€60 from Piazzale Roma to Piazza San Marco
For any crossing.

GHETTI LANDING STAGES

GONDOLAS

Venice wouldn't be Venice without its gondolas. Although it's become a purely touristic attraction, this oh-so-romantic activity is still a staple of Venice and remains one of the best ways to discover hidden treasures in the twisting city of doges. The gondoliers' trade, held in high esteem by Venetians, is handed from father to son. The price of the ride depends on the trip, although there are official fares. Expect to pay €80 for 35 minutes. Magical!

Accademia, complete
ı Venetian glass,
stal chandeliers and a
tty arch doorway. The
rooms are spacious
cozy. This is one of
most charming hotels
enice, so book well in
ance for a room
looking the Grand
al. €85–300.

a Verardo (**A** C5)
astello 4765, Campo San
po e San Giacomo; Tel.
528 61 27; casaverardo.it
tegically placed
veen the Bridge of
s and Santa Maria
nosa, this cozy hotel
16th-century *palazzo*
23 elegant rooms.
y roof terrace where
kfast is served in
mer. €90–390.

ca Locanda
ambero (**A** A4)
n Marco 4687, Calle dei
ri; Tel. 041 522 43 84
daalgambero.com
nd the Rialto market,

30 modern rooms, some of which overlook the nearby canal. The Bistrot de Venise on the ground floor serves until late at night. €90–400.

Bel Sito (**B** E2)
→ *San Marco 2517, Campo Santa Maria del Giglio Tel. 041 522 33 65 hotelbelsitovenezia.it*
Between the Grand Canal and La Fenice, 34 large and comfortable rooms with romantic 18th- and 19th-century decor. €90–350.

Do Pozzi (**B** E2)
→ *San Marco 2367, Calle Larga XXII Marzo; Tel. 041 520 78 55; hoteldopozzi.it*
A quiet hotel on a small courtyard, 200 yards from St Mark's Square. Rooms are narrow but comfortable, some overlooking the garden, others opening onto the street. Breakfast is served on the terrace in summer. Impeccable service. €80–290.

Ai due Fanali (**E** B4)
→ *Santa Croce 946, Campo di San Simeone Profeta Tel. 041 71 84 90 aiduefanali.com*
A colorful hotel on a small square that is so quiet you'd think it was private. Some of the airy, soberly decorated rooms look out onto the tree-lined campo. Pleasant terrace. €100–250.

Locanda Fiorita (**B** D1)
→ *San Marco 3457/A, Campiello Nuovo; Tel. 041 523 4754; locandafiorita.com*
A small, friendly hotel on the first floor of an ocher-colored building. The ten rooms are small but pretty. €110–190.

Santo Stefano (**B** C2)
→ *San Marco 2957, Campo Santo Stefano; Tel. 041 520 01 66; hotelsantostefano venezia.com*
A small hotel on one of the most charming squares in Venice, with 11 tastefully decorated rooms; friendly staff. €100–260.

Locanda Sturion (**D** E3)
→ *San Polo 679, Calle del Sturion; Tel. 041 523 62 43 locandasturion.com*
Exemplary, family-run three-star hotel located in a beautiful 15th-century building overlooking the Grand Canal. Luxurious rooms and a library on Venice. €100–380.

Flora (**B** E2)
→ *San Marco 2283/B, Calle Bergamaschi; Tel. 041 520 58 44; hotelflora.it*
A peaceful hotel for an enchanting stay close to St Mark's Square: pretty interior courtyard with a fountain in summer; 43 rooms. €130–395.

Ca' Pisani (**B** B3)
→ *Dorsoduro 979/A, Rio Terrà Antonio Foscarini; Tel. 041 240 14 11; capisanihotel.it*
A chic and contemporary hotel in a former 14th-

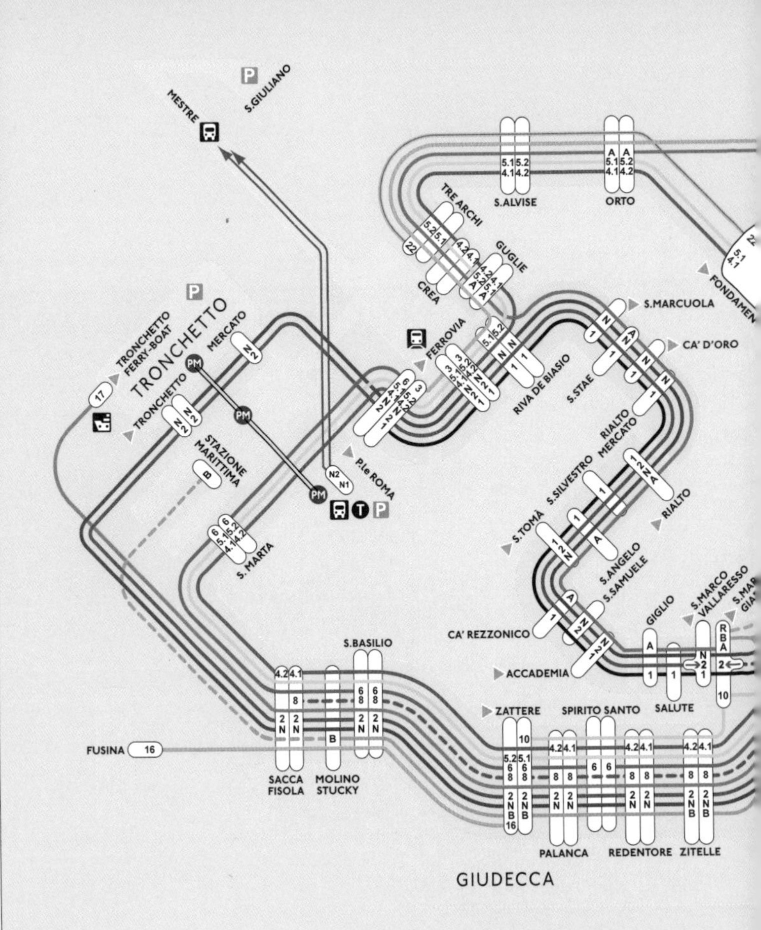

Seasonal lines

Nighttime services

Elevated shuttle train

Lagoon lines

Arancio

Blu

Rossa

Ticket sales poi

Waterbus does stop here

Waterbus stops

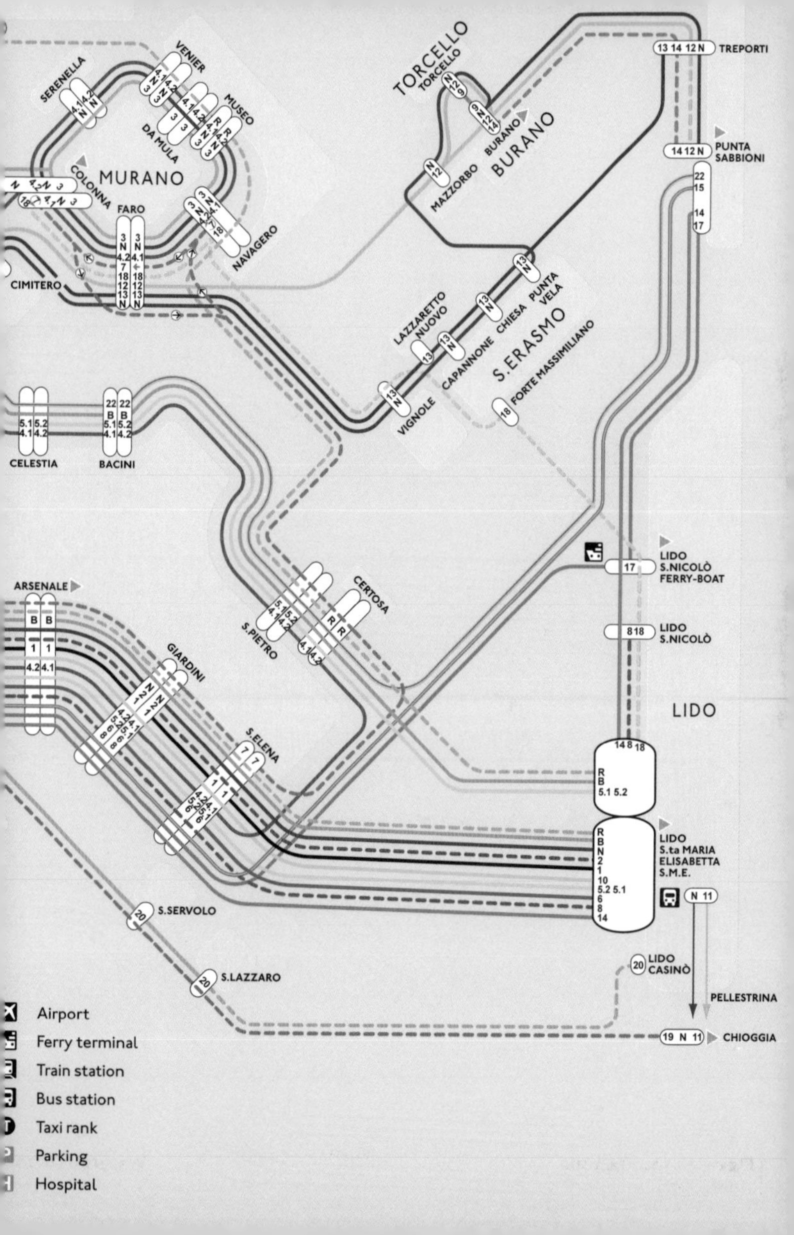
TORCELLO
TORCELLO
BURANO
BURANO
MAZZORBO
TREPORTI
PUNTA SABBIONI
MURANO
SERENELLA
VENIER
MUSEO
DA MULA
COLONNA
FARO
NAVAGERO
CIMITERO
LAZZARETTO NUOVO
CAPANNONE
CHIESA
PUNTA VELA
S.ERASMO
FORTE MASSIMILIANO
VIGNOLE
CELESTIA
BACINI
LIDO S.NICOLÒ FERRY-BOAT
LIDO S.NICOLÒ
CERTOSA
S.PIETRO
ARSENALE
GIARDINI
S.ELENA
LIDO
LIDO S.ta MARIA ELISABETTA S.M.E.
S.SERVOLO
S.LAZZARO
LIDO CASINÒ
PELLESTRINA
CHIOGGIA
Airport
Ferry terminal
Train station
Bus station
Taxi rank
Parking
Hospital

The names of streets, monuments and places to visit are followed by a map reference, the first letter of which, in bold (**A**, **B**, **C**...), refers to the corresponding area and map. The symbol ✪ refers to the Top Ten sights page at the front of the book.

Streets